Munishwar Gulati
B.E. (IIT Roorkee), A.M.I.E.,
CTO, ABES Engineering College
CEO, Siliconmedia Infocomm

Mini Gulati
B.E. (NIT, Bhopal)
CTO, Siliconmedia Infocomm

SILICON MEDIA PRESS
New Delhi

Contents

INTRODUCTION

Computer needs clear-cut instruction to tell them what to do, how to do, and when to do. A set of instructions to carry out these functions is called a program. A group of such programs that are put into a computer to operate and control its activities are called Software. These programs must reside in the internal storage (memory) to execute their instructions. For example, if we want to delete some data stored in the memory, the system uses one set of program instructions. Similarly, if we want to sort a list of names, it uses another set of instructions designed to perform the task.

Software is an essential requirement of computer systems. As a car can't run without fuel, a computer can't work without Software. There are four kinds of software that are implemented as shown in Fig.

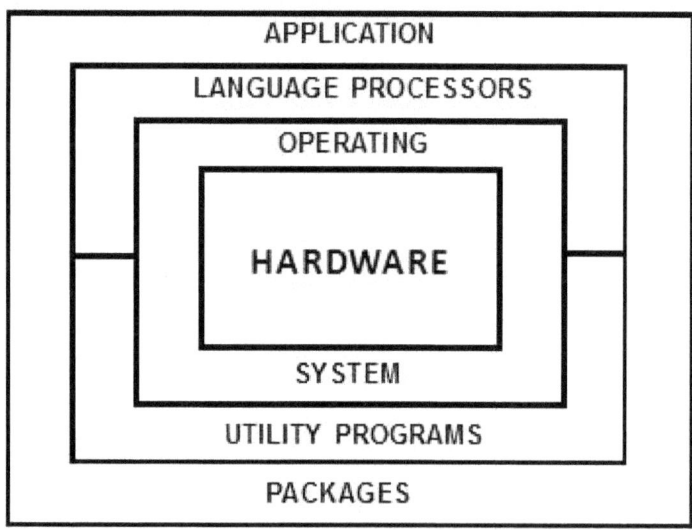

-    Operating system
-    Utility program,
-    Language processors,
-    Application programs

OPERATING SYSTEM

A Computer is a collection of parts, some mechanical, some electrical and some electronics. Getting all these parts to work together is a major problem, and that is basically what an operating system does. It manages the resources of a Computer System and schedules its operation. It provides a link between the user and the computer hardware and software.

Operating system controls nearly every aspect of the computer system. It transfers the control of computer to user and supplies the way of communicating with the computer. Thus it provides the interface between user, and Computer. The principal functions of operating system include:

-       To control and coordinate peripheral devices such as printers, display screen and disk drives.
-       To monitor the use of machine's resources.
-       To help the application programs and execute instructions.
-       To help the user to develop programs.
-       To deal with any faults that may occur in the computer and inform the user/operator.

UTILITY PROGRAM

There are many tasks common to a variety of applications. Examples of such tasks are:

-       Sorting a list in a desired sequence
-       Merging of two programs.
-       Copying a program for from one place to another.
-       Report Writing.

One need not write programs for these tasks. They are standard, and normally handled by utility programs.

```
Ex.SORT.EXE is a utility of DOS
VSAFE.EXE is virus safe utility of DOS.
```

LANGUAGE PROCESSORS

Computers can understand instructions only when they are written in their own language, called the machine language. Therefore, program written in any other language should be translated into machine language. Special programs called language processors are available to do this job.

These special programs accept the user programs and check each statement and, if it is grammatically correct, produce a corresponding set of machine code instructions. Language processors are also known as translators.

There are two kinds of translators:

-       Compilers *(COBOL, FORTRAN, C)*
-       Translators *(BASIC)*

APPLICATION PROGRAM

While an operating system makes the hardware run properly, application programs make the hardware do useful work. Applications programs are specially prepared to do certain specific tasks. They can be classified into two categories:

-       Standard Application.
-       Unique Application.

Some applications are common for many organizations. These are standard software packages and are available from hardware or software vendors.

There are situations when one may develop one's own programs to suit the requirements. Once developed, they are considered as unique applications.

```
WordStar, Lotus, dBASE are few applications
which are being widely used.
```

HISTORY OF DOS

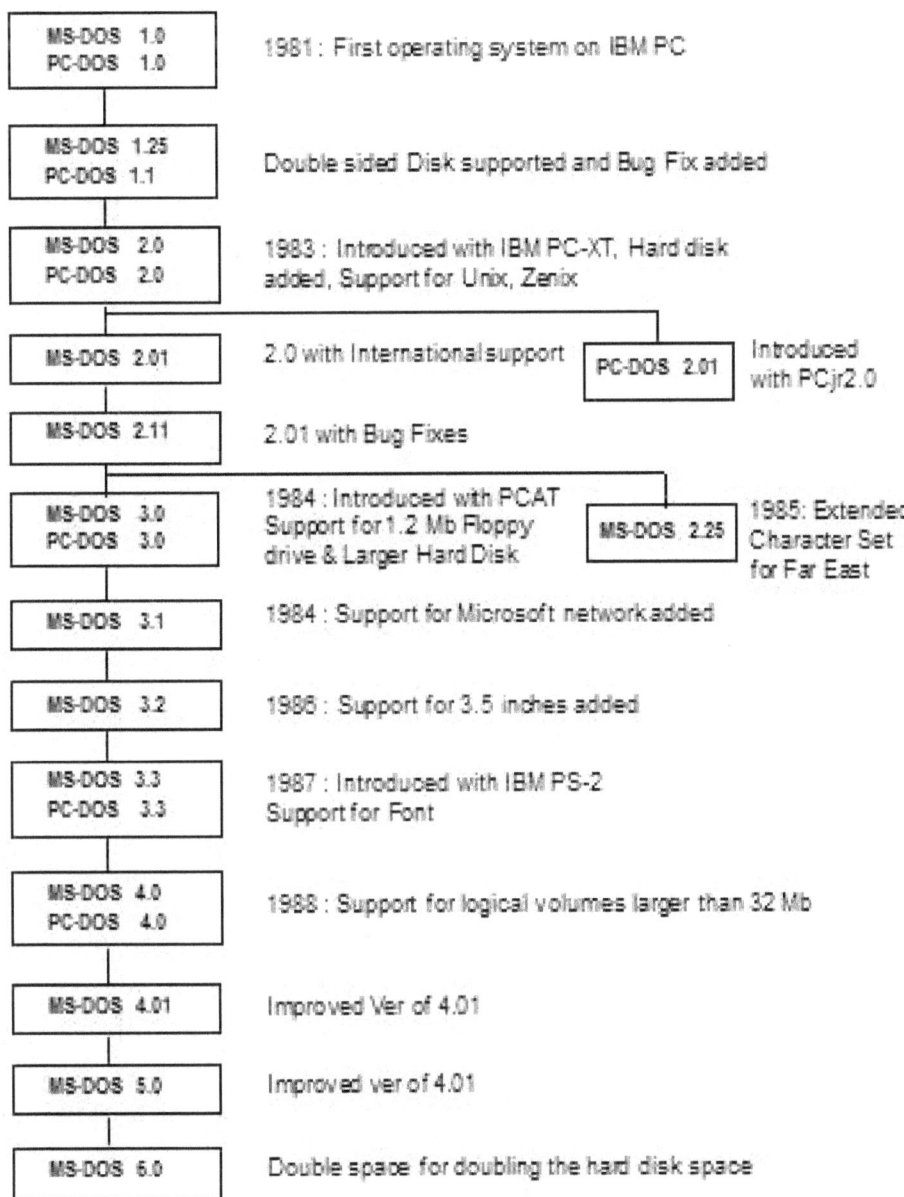

MS-DOS 1.0 PC-DOS 1.0	1981 : First operating system on IBM PC
MS-DOS 1.25 PC-DOS 1.1	Double sided Disk supported and Bug Fix added
MS-DOS 2.0 PC-DOS 2.0	1983 : Introduced with IBM PC-XT, Hard disk added, Support for Unix, Zenix
MS-DOS 2.01	2.0 with International support PC-DOS 2.01 Introduced with PCjr 2.0
MS-DOS 2.11	2.01 with Bug Fixes
MS-DOS 3.0 PC-DOS 3.0	1984 : Introduced with PCAT Support for 1.2 Mb Floppy drive & Larger Hard Disk MS-DOS 2.25 1985: Extended Character Set for Far East
MS-DOS 3.1	1984 : Support for Microsoft network added
MS-DOS 3.2	1986 : Support for 3.5 inches added
MS-DOS 3.3 PC-DOS 3.3	1987 : Introduced with IBM PS-2 Support for Font
MS-DOS 4.0 PC-DOS 4.0	1988 : Support for logical volumes larger than 32 Mb
MS-DOS 4.01	Improved Ver of 4.01
MS-DOS 5.0	Improved ver of 4.01
MS-DOS 6.0	Double space for doubling the hard disk space

5

IMPORTANCE OF OPERATING SYSTEM

The operating system is very important because it sets both the environment in which you interact with the computer and the environment in which your program work. Also the operating system sets many of the practical limits of your computer's usefulness, just as the specific hardware does.

Also, the utility programs and other application programs will not work with just any operating system and have to be generally matched to the operating system. Thus, the number of packages available for your computer is heavily influenced by the popularity of operating system that it uses.

In many ways, it doesn't matter to us if our operating system is better or worse than some other system. What does matter is how popular our operating system is.

TYPES OF OPERATING SYSTEM

Few of the most commonly used operating systems are:

- DOS
- UNIX
- CP/M-80 (CP/M-86 also)

DOS

DOS is acronym of Disk Operating System. It was pioneered by IBM and improved to the present state by Microsoft Corporation. Today, it has become the dominant operating system for the current generation of computers. In the coming topics we will discuss in detail about the MS-DOS (Microsoft-Disk Operating System).

UNIX

AT&T's Bell labs developed UNIX during a period in 1970s. It is a multi-user, multitasking operating system. The main idea behind developing UNIX was to share files and combine their individual modules into a finished program. They used high level C language to write the operating system. This made the UNIX system portable and it could now be moved to different type of computers by making some modifications and recompilation.

CP/M-80

It was the most popular operating system for 8-bit microprocessor. It enjoyed immense popularity. It's new version CP/M-86 was developed for 16/32 bit microprocessors. This operating system limits the variety and nature of devices which can be attached to the computer and kind of software which can be supported.

WHAT IS DOS?

Every computer that uses disks (hard or floppy) must have a master program that co-ordinates the flow of information from Computer to disk and from disk to Computer. Thus, it is called the Disk Operating System.

The Disk Operating System performs number of essential jobs that include:

- Controls the various applications programs, such as word processors, electronic spreadsheet, database managers etc. It creates our environment that lets these programs to talk to computer.
- Provides house-keeping and file management utilities that performs useful tasks such as

DISK OPERATIONS

FILE OPERATIONS

- Automates the repetitive task through automatic execution.

- Controls the way, the computer interpret certain commands.

- Controls the way certain information is displayed on the screen.

SOFTWARE & HARDWARE REQUIREMENTS

The various version of DOS operate with Intel's 8086, 8088, 80286, 80386, 80486 and Pentium family of microprocessors. DOS based computers are being used around the world by an estimated fifty million people for thousands of useful applications. This includes hundreds of Computer models ranging from desktop to laptop computers from nearly as many suppliers.

With a growing base of complex software programs, the need for more memory and file storage is increasing. Today it is not uncommon to find DOS-based microcomputers sporting from one to Sixty four megabytes (million characters) of memory and 50 to more than 2000 million characters of disk storage.

Your ability to take advantage of large amount of memory depends on the specific programs you use and the way you configure your computer. However, most computers using 8086, 8088, and 80286 microprocessors can't address more than 640 kB (thousand characters) of memory at a time. MS-DOS 5.0 introduced a number of important upper memory management capabilities to let user of 80286, 80386 and 80486 based microcomputers, address large portions of continuous memory above 1024 kB level, using MS-DOS 5.0, computers can load various utilities.

Until the advent of DOS 4.01, most DOS-based microcomputers were unable to address more than 32 megabytes partition of disk space at a time. DOS 4.01 eliminated the 32-megabyte barrier, giving user the ability to manage huge amounts of data on a micro technology computer.

SHORT HISTORY OF MS-DOS

MS-DOS stands for Microsoft Disk Operating System. The progenitor of MS-DOS was an operating system called 86-DOS. In July, 1981 Microsoft purchased all rights to 86-DOS made substantial alterations to it and renamed it, MS-DOS.

Till this time CP/M-80 was the most widely used operating system. Inspite of some similarities to its ancestor CP/M-80, MS-DOS version 1.0 has many advantages over CP/M80. It has an improved disk directory structure, with information about file's attributes, its size in bytes and the data on which, the file was created or last updated. This was one of the major advantages introduced over CP/M-80.

After that Microsoft continued to improve the DOS. The enclosed chart indicates the track record of DOS improvement.

STRUCTURE OF DOS

There are four essential programs associated with the control of your computer and it interacts with:

- Programs
- Keyboard and display screen
- Attached devices like drives, printers and moderns.

These are:

- Boot record
- IO.SYS
- MSDOS.SYS
- COMMAND.COM

Only COMMAND.COM program is displayed when you view a directory of filenames located on a disk. You can see the

IO.SYS and MSDOS.SYS programs by typing either dir/ah or CHKDSK/V and pressing Enter.

The purpose of system control programs is briefly defined for you in the following paragraph.

THE BOOT RECORD

The term boot or boot strap, when used with computers, means start or start up. When you boot your computer, you are tuning it on and loading the operating system into your computer's memory. This includes reading the boot record into memory, which passes the control to DOS. Next DOS checks for presence of IO.SYS and MSDOS.SYS. If these files are found, the DOS prompt is displayed on your screen. This prompt normally A > or C > depends on the active drive.

Your computer does not boot without a boot record. Instead, an error message is displayed telling you to insert a system disk. The boot record is located on track 0, Sector 1, Side 0 of your formatted DOS disk. If you have a hard disk, the boot record is located on the first sector of the first cylinder of the DOS partition.

THE IO.SYS PROGRAM

This program called, IBMBIO.COM interacts between your computer's ROM BIOS's (READ ONLY MEMORY BASIC INPUT/ OUTPUT SYSTEM) and MSDOS.SYS program. At startup IO.SYS resets the disk system and initializes attached devices. IO.SYS always contains at least five device drivers, which are used to control the operation of your keyboard, screen, printer, disk controller, and system clock.

The final task performed by IO.SYS is to load the command processor program, COMMAND.COM.

THE MSDOS.SYS PROGRAM

This program, also called IBMDOS.COM, interacts directly with applications program and the IO.SYS program described above. This program acts as the bridge between application programs and IO.SYS, as it intercepts program calls for printing, data storage or retrieval, information display, and so on, and routes these calls to the IO.SYS program, which responds to the request with the appropriate reaction.

THE COMMAND.COM PROGRAM

The COMMAND.COM Program is called the Command Processor. It intercepts, or reads, Commands from the keyboard and executable command files. These files have the filename AUTOEXEC.BAT or the file extensions .COM and .EXE. COMMAND.COM also produces the DOS disk prompt (A:\>), performs error checking, and displays error messages when system errors are detected.

BOOTING THE SYSTEM

The process of starting the computer is called booting. On MS-DOS machine the operating system is usually held on a disk, which can either be a floppy disk or a hard disk. If you have a hard disk machine, once the operating system has been installed, you usually have no need to insert the operating system disk to boot the computer.

If there is no hard disk, you need to insert the operating system disk to boot the computer. If there is no hard disk, you need to insert the operating system in the disk drive. If there are two drives, then you have to insert it into drive 'A'. The disk drive which is used to load the operating system is called default drive. As the machine boots, you will be given some information about your machine.

You can restart the computer if you ever get helplessly lost while using your computer. But it is not a good idea to restart or re-boot at the first sign of trouble. Rebooting while a program is running can damage your data, especially if you're in the middle of updating a file. Thus rebooting should be done only when there is no alternative left to you.

REBOOTING

If you must reboot your system, you have two options:

- A warm boot
- A cold boot.

WARM BOOT

It is gentler and often quicker because the computer stays powered on during the procedure. To perform a warm boot, press the key combination Ctrl+Alt+Del. To use this key combination, hold down Ctrl key then hold down Alt key, then hold the Del key. Release all the three keys after the screen clears and Computer restarts.

COLD BOOT

If a warm boot doesn't seem to clear up the problem completely, you can perform a Cold Boot. To do so, turn off the power and wait until your hard disk has stopped rotation (app. 45 sec.) And then turn the power on again.

TWO WAYS OF USING A COMPUTER (INTERACTIVE & BATCH)

When you first start using your Computer, you will probably give it your full attention. You will work with the computer interactively, which means that you do some thing and then the Computer responses. You type something else, Computer does something else. The interactive mode is one of the two fundamentals models in which the Computer can operate.

But the simple fact is when you are working with the computer interactively, the computer is keeping you busy just as much as you are keeping it busy.

When you need the computer to work at its own, unattended, then the style of computer operation is called Batch Mode.

Thus the computer can work either in interactive mode or batch mode. The difference between two is only in the attention of user required.

INSTALLING DOS 6.0

DOS 6.0 in a hefty 4 megabytes (app 4,200,000 bytes). Therefore, the harddisk on which you install DOS 6.0 must have at least that amount of free space. You can use the CHKDSK command to find out how much space is available. If you need to make room for DOS 6.0, backup your files and then delete the ones you don't want.

RUNNING SETUP

Once you are ready to install DOS 6.0, grab your DOS 6.0 setup disks, and complete the steps below:

- Insert setup Disk 1 in floppy drive A or B.
- Type A: and press <Enter>, if you have inserted the disk in drive A. (Type B: and press <Enter>, if the setup disk is in drive B:).
- Type SETUP and press <Enter>.
- SETUP will check your system configuration and make sure that there is enough space on your hard disk.
- Now a welcome screen appears which display the following message:
- Press <Enter> if you want to precede SETUP.
- Press F1 to get help before continuing.
- Press F3 twice to exit SETUP immediately.

- SETUP will check your system settings for DOS type, path & screen display. If all the settings are correct, simply press <Enter>.

- To begin installing, press Y. To cancel the installation, press F3 twice.

- Follow the screen prompts and insert the new disks as needed.

- After SETUP copies all the DOS files, it will prompt you to remove all disks from floppy drives and press <Enter>.

- Finally, SETUP will prompt you to restart the computer by pressing <Enter> again.

CREATING A DOS 6 START UP DISK

A start up disk is useful for booting a Computer that doesn't have hard disk, or as a safety valve in case you can't start your system from hard disk. To make a startup disk, grab a fresh floppy disk (formatted or unformatted) that will work in drive A. Now complete the first two steps of the setup procedure. When you go to step 3, type the command Setup/f/m and press < Enter > followed the Screen prompts to complete the remaining steps.

CONFIGURING YOUR DOS

The CONFIG.SYS and AUTOEXEC.BAT files can be used to set the way your computer responds to commands.

CONFIG.SYS

CONFIG.SYS adjusts the system configuration according to the commands contained in the file. It is loaded when booting of system taken place. It must be present on the main directory of the DOS boot disk.

AUTOEXEC.BAT

This file automatically executes the command line included within the file when system is turned on. Each command encountered in this file, runs as if the command has been typed directly from the key board Like CONFIG.SYS DOS also looks for the AUTOEXEC.BAT file during the boot process. If this file doesn't exist, the DATE & TIME prompts an automatically displayed.

    (DETAILS OF THE ABOVE FILES HAS BEEN DISCUSSED
    IN APPENDIX B)

GETTING STARTED

Before turning on your computer, DOS must be present on the boot disk. The boot disk is the primary disk from which DOS loads into computer's memory. This includes loading the boot second and DOS system files IO.SYS, MSDOS.SYS and COMMAND.COM.

If your computer has a hard disk, it is probably formatted and most likely contains all the necessary system files. If computer is only equipped with removable floppy drives, you can insert a disk containing DOS into drive A and turn on your computer.

When DOS is ready to start, it first asks for the current date and time, so it can keep track of both. The exact form in which DOS asks date and time may vary from version to version.

The most general form is

    Current date is the   1.10.1980
    Enter new date :

You can enter the date in mm-dd-yy format, using (-) hyphen to separate the month, date and year.

After typing the date, the DOS displays the same type of request for the time :

```
Current time is 0:00:12-34
Enter new time :
```

Again you can enter the time, using a colon (:) to separate hours, minutes and seconds. DOS upto 4.01 version uses 24 hr. clock, which means, that if the time is past noon, you enter a number of 12 or more. The 4.01 version and later version of DOS uses 12 hour times. Time is entered with an a or p or a.m. or p.m.

GETTING DOS TO WORK

DOS tells you that it is ready for a command by displaying what is called the DOS prompt. This literally, prompts you to type in a command.

The typical prompt looks like A> or C>, a capital letter A or C followed by a greater-than symbol. The default prompt is C, if the booting has been done from hard disk and it is A, if the booting has been done from floppy drive.

When you see the DOS prompt, probably A> or C>, then you know you are talking to DOS and it wants you to tell it what to do; it wants an instruction. The prompt is DOS's part of dialogue. To actually get DOS to do some work, you must give it a command.

Now what are commands and what can they do? In simplest terms, a command is the name of a program that you want the computer to carry out. That program/command might be the name of a program you have written, or it might be the name of a program you've bought, such as Lotus 1-2-3 or WordStar. It might be the name of a program that is a part of DOS itself or it can be the name of a special type of DOS program called a batch-execution file.

Thus the commands can be of four types:

- Your own programs
- Store bought - programs
- DOS's own programs
- DOS batch programs.

But dividing commands into four categories just gives us a way to think about them logically.

SUMMARY

A group of programs that are put into the Computer's memory to operate and control its activity are called Software.

Software can be divided into four categories basically.

Operating system - provides a link between computer hardware and software.

Utility program - Pre-written programs for performing variety of applications.

Language processors - Programs to convert any language to computer language.

Application program - Programs to perform specific tasks.

Most commonly used operating systems are

DOS (Disk Operating System) It co-ordinates the flow of information from computer to disk and from disk to Computer.

UNIX It is a multi-user, multitasking operating system. High level language C has been used to write to operating system.

CP/M-80 It was most popular for 8-bit microprocessor. It limits the verity and nature of devices which can be used with computer.

STRUCTURE OF DOS

It consist of four essential programs :

- Boot record
- IO.SYS
- MSDOS.SYS
- COMMAND.COM

BOOT RECORD

Boot means start or start up. When computer is switched on, the boot record is loaded into memory, which passes the Control to DOS.

Boot record is located on track 0, Sector 1, side 0 of the formatted disk. In hard disk it is located on first sector of first cylinder of DOS partition.

IO.SYS

Also called IBMBIO.COM in PC-DOS. It interacts between Computer's ROM BIOS's and MSDOS.SYS Program.

MSDOS.SYS

Also called IBMDOS.COM interacts directly with application program and IO.SYS file.

COMMAND.COM

Called command processor. It intercepts and reads the commands from keyboard and locate the files on the disk to execute them.

BOOTING - Process of starting the computer is called booting.

REBOOTING- is required whenever user is helplessly lost during using the computer.

WARM BOOT - Press the key combination Ctrl + Alt + Del.

COLD BOOT - is done by switching off the power and turning it on again.

INTERACTIVE MODE - It is one to one mode. In this computer executes the commands as they are typed.

BATCH MODE - Here the computer works at its own, unattended.

EXERCISE

1. In how many categories the operating system can be divided. Explain each of them in brief.

2. Why operating systems are essential requirement to operate a computer.

3. Explain the following terms -
    -   Booting
    -   Rebooting
    -   Interactive mode
    -   Batch Mode

4. How many types of operating system are there. Explain them in brief.

TRUE OR FALSE

5. Disk operating system controls the various application program.

6. UNIX is a multi-user, multitasking operating system.

7. DOS 5.0 was unable to address more than 32 MB of disk space at a time.

8. IO.SYS and MSDOS.SYS, both files are displayed when directory is viewed.

9. If there is no hard disk in the system, booting can be done with the help of floppy disk.

10. Cold booting is pressing the three keys. Ctrl+Alt+Del simultaneously.

11. In Batch processing computer can work at its own, unattended.

FILL IN THE BLANKS

12. The boot record on floppy disk is located on _____.

13. The boot record on hard disk is located at _____.

14. IO.SYS interacts between computer's _____ and _____ .

15. Process of Starting is called _____ .

16. When rebooting is done with the help of keyboard it is called _____.

17. Interactive mode is _____ (one to one/one to many) operative method.

DOS COMMANDS

DOS COMMANDS

INTERNAL & EXTERNAL DOS COMMANDS

There are two kinds of DOS commands. These are called external and Internal.

Internal commands are those commands which are loaded into memory when DOS is booted i.e. they are loaded when the three basic files IO.SYS, MSDOS.SYS and COMMAND.COM are loaded. These commands are always available for use, although no such file name or directory exists on the disk. Few internal commands are.

COPY - To copy files

DEL - To delete files

DIR - To list the files of logged drive.

External commands are conventional program files. These files can be deleted, copied and even renamed. These files are displayed when DIR command lists the directory on the screen. Few of the external commands are :

CHKDSK - Check the available space on selected disk.

DISKCOPY- To make exact copy of disks.

FEW IMPORTANT TERMS

PROGRAM

It is a series of instructions (arranged to give some meaningful result) written in Computer language. These instructions are stored in file(s) and tell computer to perform a task.

FILE

A file is a collection of information. Any information that computer stores in its permanent memory is in the file form. All computer files contain data or information and on this basis we can divide the files into two major categories:

- Program files
- Data files.

Program files are the files which can be loaded into computer's memory to tell the computer to perform a particular task. These files can be identified easily as they have extension name of .EXE or .COM.

The .COM files are under 64 KB in size and .EXE file can be over 64 KB. Both type of files can be executed by simply typing their first name.

DIRECTORY

A directory is a table of contents for a disk. It contains the names of files, size, date and time when they are last modified.

VOLUME LABEL

When you use a new disk, you can put a label on the disk to help you identify its content. Also, you can give each of your disk an internal label, called a volume label.

DISK DRIVE

Computer have external storage on disk drives (hard or floppy). The drives are identified by assigning them alphabetic letter. Letter 'C' is usually assigned to hard disk from where system is booted. Floppy drives are assigned name 'A' & 'B'. If you add more drives to your system you can assign them letters from D to Z.

FILE NAMING CONVENTIONS

Before proceeding on the DOS command let us look at the concept of a file and the file naming conventions.

A file can be looked upon as a folder containing instruction or information about some topic. Every program or set of instruction or data is stored in some file and it is assigned a name to differentiate it with others. A program is set of computer instruction collected in a file. A data file is normally a collection of characters that make up a document or database etc.

The file name in DOS has two parts :

- a primary name
- a secondary name or a file name extension.

The primary name is separated from the secondary name by a dot(.).

FILENAME RULES

- Filenames are one to eight characters in length with an option one to three character extension name. These characters must not br seperated by any space.
- Filename can include any of the following characters A-Z or a-z, 0-9, $, &, #, @ ! % ' ( ) . { } -
- Other characters such as :, ; | + / \ are not allowed as they have special meaning.
- Reserved device names are not allowed.
- A period is used to separate the first part of a file name from extension.
- The extension name like .EXE, .COM and .BAT are given special status by DOS. These files are called executable files and are in a form which can be understood by the machine.

CHANGING THE CURRENT DRIVE

The current drive tells DOS where to look for files and directories. If the files or directories, you want to work with are located on the current drive, You don't have to specify the drive when typing commands. If the files or directories aren't on the current drive, you must specify the drive you want.

To change the current drive, from the command and prompt, type the drive letter, a colon, and press <Enter>. Thus to change the default drive to floppy disk in drive A, you would place a disk in drive A and then type A : or a : and press < Enter >.

DIR COMMAND [INTERNAL]

DIR Command is used to display filenames on your screen. It displays the disk's volume label and serial number, on directory or filename per line, including the filename extension, the file size in bytes, and the date and time, the file was last modified.

If you simply type DIR it displays the directory of the default drive.

DIR Commands also reports about the total space used by the files in bytes and the amount of the space left free (also in byte) remaining on the disk.

Syntax

DIR [drive:] [Path][filename] [/P] [/W] [/A [[:] attributes]] [/0 [[:] sort order]] [/S] [/B] [/L] [/C]

Parameters

[drive:][Path] - Specifies the drive and directory for which you want to see a listing.

[filename] - Specifies a particular file or group of files for which you want to see a listing.

Switches

/P   Displays one Screen of the listing at a time. To see the next screen press any key.

27

/W   Displays the listing in wide format with as many as five filenames or directory names in one line. This way it omits file size, date and time.

/A [{:} attributes]

     Displays only the names of those directories and files with the attributes you specify N>P> If you omit this switch, DIR displays the names of all files except hidden files and system files.

     If this switch is added without the attributes, DIR displays the name of all the files, hidden files and System files.

Attributes

H	Hidden files
-H	files that are not hidden
S	system files
-S	files other than system files.
D	Directories
-D	Files only (not directory)
A	files ready for achieving
-A	Files that have not changed since the last backup
R	Read only files
-R	Files that are not read-only.

/O[(:) sort order]

     Controls the order in which DIR sorts and display directory names and filenames. If you omit this switch, DIR displays the names in the order in which they occur in the directory. If you use this switch without specifying sort order, DIR displays the names of the directories, sorted in alphabetic order, then displays the file, sorted in alphabetic order.

Sort order

N	In alphabetic order
-N	In reverse alphabetic order
E	In alphabetic order by extension
-E	In reverse alphabetic order by extension.
D	By date and time, earliest first.
-D	by date and time, latest first
G	with directories grouped before files.
-G	With directories grouped after files.
C	By compression ratio, lowest first.
-C	By compression ratio, highest first.
/S	List every occurrence, in the specified directory and all sub-directories of the specified file name.

/B	Lists each directory name or filename, one per line (including the filename extension). This switch displays no heading information and no summary.
/L	Displays unsorted directory names and filenames in lower case.
/C	Displays the compression ratio of files.

Example

DIR/P/W	directory widthwise & pagewise.
DIR/AD	displays only directories.
DIR/AH	displays only the hidden files.
DIR/O-D	displays the directory sorted on, date and time, latest first.
DIR A:	displays the directories of A drive.

Standard output of DIR command is :

Volume in drive C is MS-DOS_6

Volume Serial Number is 0021-003D

```
     Directory of C:\
COMMAND COM        54,645        05-31-94  6:22a
DOS          <DIR>                01-01-80  12:01a
WINA20       386      9,349       05-31-94  6:22a
CONFIG       SYS      36          01-01-80  12:32a
AUTOEXEC     BAT      54          01-01-80  12:32a
FOXBASE      <DIR>                01-01-80  12:00a
WS           <DIR>                01-01-80  12:03a
        8 file(s)  64,084 bytes
             25,407,488 bytes free
```

WILD CARD AND LITERAL

Wild cards are useful when you have to refer to a family of files instead of a single file. In DOS, an asterisk (*) character is "wild". It stands for one or more characters in a filename or extension, beginning with the asterisk position. If only an asterisk is used, it represents the entire filename.

- DIR *.COM.displays all files which has COM as its extension name.
- DIR W*display all files starting with W and having any extension.
- DIR WA*.*displays all files starting with WA and having any extension.
- The wild card *.* stands for all files names and all extension and pronounced as star dot star.

LITERAL

The question mark (?) is used within filenames and extension to represent any single character.

DIR D???????.???Displays all the files starting with D and having any extension.

DIR D???.*Displays all the files starting with D and having less than four characters in file name and any extension.

DIR A???.??Displays all the files starting with letter A, having four or less characters in file names and having two or less characters in extension name.

VOL COMMAND[INTERNAL]

The volume command displays the volume label of the current disk. Simply type VOL and press Enter to display the label.

Syntax

VOL

Volume in drive C is HILTRON

Volume Serial Number is 0021-003D

LABEL COMMAND [INTERNAL]

The label command is used to create, change or delete the volume label on a disk. Whereas the VOL command only displays the label, the label command can display and change the label.

Syntax

LABEL C:< label name >

If you simply type Label at the DOS prompt it displays the following message.

Volume in drive C is HILTRON

Volume Serial Number is 0021-003D

Volume Label (11 character, Enter for none) ?-

You can type the new name of maximum 11 characters and press Enter.

Pressing enter without typing a new volume label delete the existing volume label, but before deleting it gives precautionary prompt that reads

"Delete Current volume label [Y/N] ?"

This gives you a final chance to change your mind. Y and Enter deletes the label name which N & Enter keeps it.

You can directly change the label by typing the new label name along with label command.

DATE & TIME

When the system booting is done, after loading all the essential files in the memory, it prompt for current date and current time as discussed earlier. If you simply press Enter at that point, the system takes the default date and time.

DATE COMMAND[INTERNAL]

To change the date when DOS is already loaded in the memory this command is used.

Syntax

DATE (mm-dd-yy)

If simple DATE command is entered it displays the following prompt :

Current date is 01.01.1980

Enter new date (mm-dd-yy) :

You can respond by typing the new date.

Without displaying the above prompt, if the date is to be changed simply type date followed by new date.

DATE 03-01-95

Here the value of the date, month and year can be separated by periods (-), hyphens (-), or Slash marks (/). The valid values for mm, dd & yy are

mm   01 through 12

dd   01 through 31

yy   80 through 99 or 1980 through 2099

TIME COMMAND [INTERNAL]

Like the DATE command, TIME command can also be changed even after loading DOS into memory.

Syntax

TIME [hours:(minutes{:seconds.(.hundredths)}] (A:P)]

If only TIME is typed and entered at DOS prompt it displays the following prompt

Current time is 12:22:38.08a

Enter new time :

You can respond by typing new time. If you want to change the time without displaying the prompt, simply type TIME followed by the new valid time.

TIME 02:22:02.23a

The valid values of parameters are :

hours	**0 through 23**
minutes	**0 through 59**
seconds	**0 through 59**
hundredths	**0 through 99**

A:Pspecifies A.M. or P>M> for the 12-hour time format. If you type a valid 12-hr time but do not type A or P, time uses A (a.m.).

VER COMMAND[INTERNAL}

It displays the MS-DOS version number

Syntax VER

When you Enter VER command, MS-DOS displays the following message.

MS-DOS Version 6.0

CHKDSK COMMAND[EXTERNAL]

It checks the status of a disk and displays the status report, which include several important items.

- The total disk space

- The total disk space occupied and number of files.

- The total disk space either lost or considered unusable by the system.

- The amount of disk space available for use.

- The total amount of memory available in your Computer.

- The amount of memory occupied by the operating system.

- The amount of memory available for use.

It also shows error found in MS-DOS filing system, which consist of file allocation table (FAT) and directories.

Syntax

CHKDSK [drive:] [(path) filename] [/F] [/V]

If you only type CHKDSK, it displays the status of logged drive.

Parameters

Drives: Specifies the drive that contains the disk that you want CHKDSK to check.

Path [Filename]

Specifies the location and name of a file or set of files that you want CHKDSK to check for fragmentation. You can use wild cards (* and ?) to specify multiple files.

Switches

/F   Fixed errors on the disk.

/V   displays the name of each file in every directory as the disk is checked.

CLS COMMAND[INTERNAL]

It clears the screen. It cleared screen shows only the command prompt and cursor at top left corner.

Syntax

CLS

DISK PREPARATION COMMANDS

FORMAT COMMAND[EXTERNAL]

A brand new diskette is just like a blank paper. As rules are required to write onto the paper to write something on it, cerain guidelines are required by DOS to write onto these disks. Formatting creates this framework - the guidelines for DOS to use in writing on your disks. Datas and files can be written or copied onto a formatted diskettes, but not on unformatted diskettes.

Format actually does two important things with a diskette:

- It draws the electronic "rules" that makes it possible for DOS to work with the diskette .

- It checks for any defects in the diskette, because diskettes are so vulnerable, they may have damaged patches on them. But a diskette with a bad patch can still be used - the FORMAT command knows how to recognize these bad patches and put up a safety fence around them.

Syntax

FORMAT target: /switches

FORMAT requires that you specify a drive letter for the disk to format.

When you run the format command, it displays a message indicating the drive you are about to format, and prompts you to press <Enter> when ready to proceed. This gives you the oppurtunity to change the disk in the drive if necessary, or cancel the operation by pressing Ctrl + C.

When formatting operation is complete, DOS displays a message showing the total number of bytes available on disk, how many bytes have been marked as "bad sectors" and how many bytes have been used in system files. It also prompts you to enter the volume label before asking for repeating the format procedure. If you enter Y, you are prompted to enter another disk and press another disk, otherwise you are returned to the DOS prompt.

Switches

/1	Format a double sided disk as single sided disk.
/4	Formats a single-density (160 kB) or a double density (360 kB) with the correct number of tracks & sectors.
/8	Formats 8 sectors per track instead of default, 9sectors per track.
/B	Formats a disk so as to leave room for the system files, although system files are not copied.
/F:size	Specifies the size, in kilobytes, of the disk to be formatted. Not to be used with /1, /8, /T or / N options. The following sizes can be used :

160 kB= 5.25" single sided, 8 sectors/track

180 kB= 5.25" single sided, 9 sectors/track

320 kB= 5.25" double sided, 8 sectors/track

360 kB= 5.25" double sided, 9 sectors/track

720 kB= 3.5" double sided, 9 sectors/track

1.2 MB= 5.25" high density, 15 sectors/track

1.44 MB= 3.5" high density, 15 sectors/track

2.88 MB= 3.5" extra high density, 30 sectors/ track

/N:nn	Indicates the number of sectors per track, where nn is the number of sectors you specify. This must be used with /T option.
/Q	Specifies that formatting does not reinitialize tracks and sectors on a previously formatted disk.
/S	Transfers DOS system files to the formatted disk. Intended to make a disk "bootable" - that is capable of loading DOS into memory when the computer is booted up while the disk is in the default boot drive.
/T:nn	Indicates the number of tracks on the disk, where nn is the number of tracks you specify.
/U	Specifies unconditional reformatting. All data on the previosly formatted disk is destroyed, and you will not be able to unformat this disk later.
/V	Prompts you to add the volume label to the disk after formatting. A volume label is a string, upto 11 characters long, that can function as an identifying tittle for the disk.
/V:Label	Automatically adds the defined volume label to the disk after formatting.

E.g.   Format A:/S/V

Formats a disk in drive A, using current drive defaults, then copies the system files to the disk. and prompts the user to enter a volume label for the disk.

Format A:/F:360K

Formats a 5.25" double-density (360KB) disk in a high density drive (1.2 MB).

SYS COMMAND[EXTERNAL]

It copies the DOS system files to a new disk.

Syntax

SYS target:

SYS transfers the DOS system files (IO.SYS & MSDOS.SYS), plus the COMMAND.COM file, to a formatted disk without requiring formatting.

A target drive must be specified where SYS is to place the operating system files. Also you can include a source drive and path where DOS can locate the system files, before specifying the target.

E.g.SYS A:

Copies files from the currently logged drive to A drive.

SYS C: A:

Copies system files to drive A from drive C, even if you are not logged on drive C. The file SYS.COM must be available on the currently logged drive.

WORKING WITH DIRECTORIES

All disks, whether floppy or hard, have fixed size directory of files. This is called that root or main directory. This isn't the only directory a disk can have, though. The disk's root directory can have sub-directories under it and each of those can have any mixture of files and sub-directories under it.

Each new directory branches out from its parent directory, and each one in turn can have any number of other sub-directories under it.

In a multiple level directory structure, the different directories can be looked upon as filling cabinets. Each filling cabinet consists of files, containing information pertaining to particular topic.

THE ROOT DIRECTORY

The first level in a multilevel directory is the root directory, which is created automatically when a disk is formatted, and files are added to it. More directories & sub-directories can be created with-in the root directory.

NEED OF SUB-DIRECTORY

Sub-directories are intended for use with the fast speed and huge capacity of a hard disk system. Unless you have a lot of files on the disk, then is little need for organizing them in isolated group. But having similar and related files together makes it easier and faster to use them.

You can create as many sub-directories as you need, but make your directory structure as simple as possible. All the sub-directories should be placed onto the root directory of the disk and unless there is a really good reason, the branches should not be created off any other directory than the roof.

PATHS TO A DIRECTORY

The way to a particular sub-directory on a disk is referred as a path. A path is the root that traces the way from a disk's root directory, out to some point in the branching directory tree. The description of the path is called the path name.

The following diagram explains the multilevel directory structure and path.

As is clear from the above hierarchy, a multilevel directory structure can be thought of as a tree structure. Directories can be considered as branches of the tree and files as the leaves.

Here SONE, STWO & STHREE are the three sub-directories of the root and FILEI is also at the root. Thus ROOT can be considered as parent dir of SONE, STWO and STHREE sub-directories. Similarly SONE is parent directory of SONE and STHREE is parent directory of SSTHREE.

The path to any sub-directory or file starts from ROOT. Let us take the case of FILE3.

- To reach to FILE3, find the sub-directory SONE.
- Find the sub-directory SSONE of SONE.
- Find the FILE3 in sub-directory SSONE.

All the above can be replaced by with a short and simple reverse slash (\) thus the path description of FILE3 can be described as

\SONE\SSONE\FILE3.

MD (MAKE DIRECTORY) COMMAND [INTERNAL]

To create a new directory, you use the MKDIR or MD command followed by the name of the sub-directory.

Syntax

MKDIR drive :path

MDdrive :path

Drive :

Specifies the drive (if other than current drive) on which you want to create the new directory.

Path :   Specifies the name and location of the new directory. The maximum length of any single path from the root directory to the new directory is 63 characters including back slashes (\).

When a directory is created, it is empty except for two reference entries, a single dot (.) and a double dot (..) which DOS uses as markers to tell it where it is and where it comes from.

After creating a directory, files can be placed in it. All names in one directory - name of files or name of sub-directories must be unique within the directory, but the same names can be used in other directories.

E.g.To create a directory COBOL at root type

MD COBOL

If a sub-directory is to be added to the existing directory, it is required to include the path to the new directory in the command.

To create a sub-directory PROJECT of COBOL use the command

MD COBOL\PROJECT

RD (REMOVE DIRECTORY) COMMAND [INTERNAL]

It removes or deletes a sub-directory. But before you can delete a directory, all the files and sub-directories must be removed. The directory must be empty except for "." and ".." symbols.

Syntax

RMDIR (drive:) path

RD(drive:) path

(drive:)path

Specifies the location and name of the directory you want to delete.

If you try to delete a directory that contains any file or sub-directories except "." and "..", DOS displays the message

Invalid path, not directory,

or directory not empty.

Also to remove the sub-directory, it is required to give the RD Command at parent directory because no directory can be removed while staying in it.

TREE COMMAND[EXTERNAL]

Since a disk can have numerous sub-directories branching out from the root directory, you need a way of finding out what all the branches of the tree are. It displays the structure of a directory graphically.

Syntax

TREE (drive:) (path) (/F) (/A)

Parameters

Drive :   Specifies the drive (other than current drive) that contains the disk for which you want to display the directory structure.

Path :   Specifies the directory for which you want to display the directory structure.

Switches:

/F   Displays the names of the files in each directory.

/A   Specifies that TREE is to use text characters instead of graphic characters to show the lines linking sub-directories.

In the example taken if TREE Command is given it will display as follows :

C:.

COBOL

PROJECT

CD (CHANGE DIRECTORY) COMMAND[INTERNAL]

It would be a nuisance to keep typing the lengthy path name for every command if some commands are to be used from various files in the sub-directory. DOS always assumes that the command given is associated with the current directory unless it is specified by PATH Command.

To change the current directory or to make any sub-directory as current directory, CD command can be used / It takes the control to the changed directory.

Syntax

CHDIR (drive:) (path)

CHDIR(..)

CHDIR (\)

CD(drive:) (path)

CD (..)

CD (\)

to display the current drive letter and directory name, use either of the following Syntax line

CHDIR

CD

Parameters

(drive:) pathSpecifies the drive (if other than the current drive) and directory to which you want to change.

..   Specifies that you want to change to parent directory.

\   Specifies that you want to change to root directory.

In the example taken, to change the current directory to PROJECT Sub-directory type the command :

CD \ COBOL \ PROJECT

To go back to root the command will be

CD

If you ever forget which sub-directory you're in, the command CD with no parameters tells DOS to let you know for example, if you type CD in PROJECT Sub-directory, DOS displays

\COBOL\PROJECT

PATHS & PROGRAMS

The programs are stored on disk in form of files in different sub-directories.

When DOS is asked to look for a program, it looks only at one place : the current directory.

Now to execute a program, DOS must be able to locate the concerned file. If DOS doesn't find it in the current directory, it will search in as many other places as you have told it to do. PATH Command is used to extend the search in other sub-directories.

PATH COMMAND [INTERNAL]

It is used to provide access to files located in other directories or on other disks.

Syntax

PATH [(drive:) path (;......)]

To display the current search path, use the following syntax:

PATH

To clear all search path settings other than the default setting (the current directory), use the following syntax

PATH ;

Parameters

(drive:) path   Specifies a drive, directory and any sub-directories to search.

;   When used as the only parameter, clears all search path settings and specifies that MS-DOS is to search only the current directory.

To illustrate PATH Command, assume you have a program LEARN.COM which is located in a sub-directory PROJECT of directory COBOL (at root).

Here to set-up search for LEARN.COB, you can specify the disk and directories using the PATH Command. Enter the following command line at DOS Prompt.

PATH   \COBOL\PROJECT.

Now the DOS will search for the given command in the current directory and in PROJECT Sub-directory of COBOL.

You can type PATH Command to display the path setup. To do this type PATH & Press Enter.

C> PATH

PATH =\COBOL\PROJECT

To cancel the path setting give the following command.

Now if you check the path set up with PATH Command, the message "No Path" is displayed.

C >PATH;

C > PATH

No Path.

PROMPT COMMAND [INTERNAL]

When DOS is ready for a command, it shows a prompt, which is normally C> or A>, but you can change the prompt to nearly anything, including a display of current time and date with PROMPT Command.

Suppose you want the prompt to appear as HILTRON instead of C> or A>, then type the following Command :

C > PROMPT HILTRON <Enter>

45

HILTRON <Enter>

HILTRON

If you want to go back to default prompt, simply type PROMPT & Press Enter.

HILTRON PROMPT <Enter>

C>

Sometimes, the PROMPT Command proves to be very useful. If, while working in sub-directories, you lose track of when you are and what the current directory is, you can type CD to find out where you are. But if you have to change the directories very frequently, then it becomes cumbersome to check the current directory again and again.

In such cases, the directory prompt command ensures that the name of current directory always appears.

To change the DOS prompt (C> or A>) to directory prompt command use the following command :

C > PROMPT PG

Here $P command ensures the appearance of directory name and $G command ensures the appearance of '>' sign. The other combination of command prompt are described below :

$Q= (equal sign)

$$$ (dollar sign)

$TCurrent time

$DCurrent date

$PCurrent drive 8 Path

$VMS DOS-Version number

$NCurrent drive

$G> (greater than sign)

$L<(less than sign)

$B| (pipe)

$-Enter-Linefeed

$EASCII Escape Code (Code 27)

$HBackspace

Suppose your current directory is COBOL.

Following examples illustrates commands and resulting prompts.

C>PROMPT PG

C:\COBOL>PROMPT PD

C:\COBOLWed 01.02.95 PROMPT PV

C:\COBOL16:28:07.95 PROMPT PV

C:\COBOLMS-DOS Version 6.00 PROMPT $P$$

C:\COBOL$ PROMPT PB

C:\COBOL| PROMPT PL

C:\COBOL< PROMPT P-

C:\COBOL

PROMPT P

C:\COBOL PROMPT COMMAND?

COMMAND? PROMPT PG

C:\COBOL>PROMPT NG

C>

If you give a character following $ which is unrecognizable by DOS, it is ignored and not displayed.

DELTREE COMMAND (EXTERNAL)

The DELTREE Command introduced in DOS 6.0, is used to delete an entire directory structure. It deletes a directory and all the files and sub-directories that are in it.

Syntax

DELTREE (/Y) (drive:) path [(drive:) Path (....)]

Parameter

Drive: Path   Specifies the name of the directory you want to delete. The DELTREE Command will delete all the files contained in the directory you specify, as well as all the sub-directories and files in the sub-directories -subordinate to this directory.

Switch:

/Y   carries out DELTREE command without first prompting you to confirm the deletion.

COPYING FILES & DISKS

Most of the work that is done in DOS is related to disks and files on them. It is time to learn about the most fundamental and useful command you can use with your disk files. Most of the time, it is required to create new files, make duplicate copies of the file, get rid of unwanted files, display them, change their names and compare them to see if two files are same.

FILES

Most of the work that is done in DOS is related to disks and files on them. It is time to learn about the most fundamental and useful command you can use with your disk files. Most of the time it is required to create new files, make duplicate copies of the file, get ride unwanted files, display them, change their names and compare them to see if two files are same.

COPY CON COMMAND[INTERNAL]

This command is used to create new files. You can type any matter in the new file, but the last character must be ctrl-Z or F6 which is recognized by the DOS as an end-of-file marker.

Here, one thing is important. Each line in the file is completed by pressing < Enter > and once <Enter> is pressed, the line can't be modified. So no editing can take place in the typed matter.

Syntax

COPY CON NEWNAME

Ex. C> Copy CON FILE1

This is file number one.

It contains three lines.

This is the last line

^ Z

The above command created a file FILE1 with the above matter typed in it.

COPY COMMAND[INTERNAL]

Copy command starts out as something very simple, a tool to make copies of the disk file. It is used to :

-     Copy one or more specified files to another disk with the same filename, date and time information.

-     Copy one or more specified files to the same or to another disk with a different filename.

-     Copy one or more specified files to the same or to another disk with the current system date and time.

-     Concatenate (or combine) two or more files into a single file.

-     Create a new file by copying what is typed on the screen (CON:) to a designated file.

Syntax

COPY [/Y |/ -Y] [/A |/B] Source [/A|/b]]+.....] Destination [/A|/B] [/V]

Source :   Specifies the location and name of a file or set of files from which you want to copy. Source can consist of a drive letter and colon, a directory name, a filename or a combination destination.

Destination: Specifies the location and name, of a file or set of files to which you want to copy. Destination can consist of a drive letter and colon, a directory name, a filename or a combination.

Switches :

/Y	Indicates that you want copy to replace existing file(s) without prompting you for confirmation. By default, if you specify an existing file as the destination file, copy will ask you if you want to overwrite the existing file.
/-Y	Indicates that you want copy to prompt you for confirmation when replacing an existing file. Specifying this switch overrides all defaults.
/A	Indicates an ASCII text file.
/B	Indicates a binary file.
/V	Verifies that new files are written correctly.

The most general form of copy command is COPY source file target file.

Ex. COPY C:\ COBOL\PROJECT\ABC.COB   A:\ABCI.COB.

This command copies the file ABC COB from the sub-directory PROJECT to disk A with a new file name ABC1.COB.

It is only necessary to specify a target file name if you want to change the filename, otherwise the existing filename is used.

Following list illustrates the other forms of COPY Command.

COPY OLDNAME NEWNAME

-       Makes a copy of the file OLDNAME on the active disk drive. The copied file is given the NEW NAME.,

50

COPY OLDNAME B :

- Makes a copy of the file OLDNAME on the active disk drive and places it on the disk in drive B. The copy retains the original name, date and time information.

COPY OLDNAME B:/V

- Makes a copy of the file OLDNAME on the active disk drive and places it on the disk in drive B as in the previous example. The /V parameter verifies the integrity of the data as it is copied.

COPY B:MYWORDS.TXT A :

- Makes a copy of file MYWORD.TXT from drive B to drive A. with the original filename, date and time.

COPY OLDNAME B:NEWNAME

- Makes a copy of the file OLDNAME which is located in the active disk drive, and places it on the disk in drive B with the filename NEWNAME.TXT.

COPY STUFF.TXT+THINGS.TXT NEW.TEX

- Combines the files STUFF.TXT plus THINGS.TXT into a new file named NEW.TXT. The new file NEW.TXT is given the current date and time. You can combine many files this way.

COPY FIRST+SECOND+THIRD+FOURTH

- Adds the names files to the end of the FIRST file. The result is copied to the FIRSTFILE.

COPY *.TXT ALL.TXT

- Copies all files having .TXT extension into the file named ALL.TXT.

COPY *.TXT+*.COB ONE.TXT

- Copies all files having .TXT and .COB extension into one file named ONE.TXT.

COPY HANDY.TXT *.TXT

- Copies all files having the .TXT extension (except HANDY.TXT.) to the end of the file HANDY.TXT.

COPY *.* \TEXT

- Copies all files in the active directory to the directory having the path name TEXT. You can substitute a period (.) for *.*. The period (.) represents all the filenames in the parent directory.

COPY *.* \

- Copies all files in the active directory to the parent directory.

ERASE OR DEL COMMAND[EXTERNAL]

If the duplicates copies of the file can be created by copy command, it may be required sometime to delete or remove some files. For that operation, there is DEL/ERASE command. This is one command but with two different names; DEL or delete and ERASE for erase. Either command name will cause DOS to throw a file away.

You can remove files one at a time, using wild card file names. In the latter case, there is a risk of mistakable telling the DOS, to delete all files by using *.*. To protect you from that one possibility, DEL/ERASE will pause to ask whether you are sure or Not. It displays

"Are you Sure (Y/N)" ?

That is your only chance to back out. Typing 'Y' followed by <Enter> will bring the disaster.

Syntax

DEL (drive:) (path) filename [/P]
ERASE (drive:) (path) filename [/P]

Parameter

[Drive:] [path] filename

>Specifies the location and name of the file or set of files you want to delete.

Switch

/P >Prompts you for confirmation before deleting the specified file.

REN COMMAND[INTERNAL]

The RENAME COMMAND is used to change the name of one or more files. The RENAME Command is straight forward and easy to use.

You can rename all the files matching the specified filename. You cannot use the RENAME command to rename files across drives or to move files to a different directory location.

Syntax

RENAME [drive:] [path] filename1 filename2

REN [drive:] [path] filename1 filename2

Parameters

[drive:] [path] filename1

>Specifies the location and name of the file or set of files you want to rename.,

Filename2 >Specifies the new name for the file or,, if you use wild cards, the new names for the files.

Few examples of REN command are illustrated below.

REN B:OLDNAME NEWNAME

- >This changes the file OLDNAME located on B drive to NEWNAME.

REN *.* *.COB

- This changes the extension PRG to COB on all filenames located on the disk in the default drive.

TYPE COMMAND [INTERNAL]

The type command displays the contents of standard text (ASCII) files on your screen. It is the handy way to get a quick look at the contents of a file. In fact, TYPE is really just a COPY Command with the target of the COPY being your display screen instead of another file.

Syntax

TYPE < filename >

If you tell DOS to display a file that is not a text file, you may be surprised to see and hear a string of indecipherable symbols and strange beeps.

If you want to display and print a file simultaneously, you can press ctrl-P or (Ctrl-PrtScr.) prior to pressing < Enter > at the end of the TYPE command line.

MOVE COMMAND [EXTERNAL]

MOVE Command is used to move one or more files to another drive or directory location and allows you to rename directories.

It has the same effect as copying a file to a new location and then deleting the file in the original location, in a single command. You can rename a file as you move it by specifying a new name for the file.

Any file in the target location that has the same name as a source file is automatically overwritten.

You can rename a directory using the MOVE Command by specifying the old directory name as the source and new directory name as target.

Syntax

MOVE Source:\Path\file(s) target\path\file(s)

Ex.   MOVE C:\COBOL*.*C:\PROJECT

The above command Moves all the file from C:\COBOL to C:\PROJECT. Here *.* includes all files and extensions. Here \PROJECT is the target directory. If it exist, the files are moved to it. If \PROJECT doesn't exist, the MOVE Command creates it.

DISKCOPY COMMAND [EXTERNAL]

This commands makes an verbatim copy of one removable disk (source disk) on another (target disk). The involved diskettes must be of the same size. If the target disk is not formatted, DISKCOPY will automatically format it for you.

Syntax

DISKCOPY (Source: (target:)) (/I) (/V)

Parameters

Source :   Drive containing the disk to be copied ; if omitted, the current drive is assumed.

Target :   Drive that is to receive the copy; if omitted, the current drive is assumed.

Switches

/1   Copies only the first side of the disk.

/V   Verifies that the copy is correct. This slows the copy process.

When copying is complete, the prompt "COPY another (y/ N) ?" is displayed. Typing N discontinues the DISKCOPY process and returns to the system prompt. Typing Y lets you repeat the DISKCOPY Command, allowing you to make multiple copies of the sourcedisk.

SUMMARY

- Internal DOS Commands are those commands which are loaded into memory, when DOS is loaded. It is loaded with three basic files IO.SYS, MSDOS.SYS and COMMAND.COM.

- External Commands : There are conventional program files. Each external command requires its separate executable file, which must by physically present on the disk to let the command to execute.

- File naming convention :

  The file name in DOS has two parts :

  - a primary name

  - a file name extension.

- File names are one to eight character in length with an option of one to three characters of option name. The two are separated by dot.

- DIR   Displays the list of files in a directory.

- WILD CARDa Single asterisk (*) stands for one or more character on file name directory name on extension.

- LITERAL(?)   To represent any single character in file name, extension name or directory name.

- VOL   Displays the Disk volume Label.

- LABEL   Adds or modifies disk volume label.

- DATE   Displays or sets the system date.

- TIME   Displays or sets the system time.

- VER   Displays the MS-DOS version number

- CHKDSK   Checks the status of the disk and displays status report.

- CLS   Clears the screen.

-	FORMAT	Prepares a blank disk for receiving and storing data, or creates a new blank disk from a used one.
-	SYS	Copies the DOS system files to a new disk.
-	MD	Creates a new sub-directory.
-	RD	Removes or deletes a sub-directory
-	CD	Displays or changes the currently logged sub-directory.
-	TREE	Displays the structure of a directory graphically.
-	PATH	Specifies a list of sub-directories where DOS is to search for executable program files.
-	PROMPT	Changes the appearance of a DOS system prompt.
-	DELTREE	Removes a directory, including all its files and sub-directories.
-	COPY CON	Used to create new file.
-	COPY	Copies and combine files.
-	ERASE, DEL	Deletes files.
-	REN	Renames files fully
-	TYPE	Displays the content of a file.
-	MOVE	Moves a file from one place to another.
-	DISKCOPY	Makes a verbatim copy of removable disk on another disk.
-	FILTERS	Can process the information in unique way as data pass through it.

EXERCISE

OBJECTIVE TYPE QUESTIONS

1. External commands
    a) Require special DOS files
    b) Can be executed without special files.
    c) Any of the above.
    d) None of the above.

2. Which of the following filenames are valid -
    a) HILTRON.DBF   b) EXP?A.COM.
    c) XCOPY.EXE   d) A????.COM.

3. When DIR command is given on DOS prompt, it displays
    a) Name of file or directory
    b) Number of bytes used.
    c) Number of bytes free.
    d) date of file creation.
    e) time of file creation.
    f) Volume label.
    g) No. of files
    h) all of above.

4. DOS displays the date in the format
    a) DD/MM/YY   b) YYYY/DD/MM
    c) MM/DD/YY   d) MM-DD-YY

5. FORMAT A:/F:360K/S will do the following job -
    a) It will format a 5.25" double density diskette, in High density drive creating 9 sectors/track and will make the disk bootable.
    b) It will format a 3.5" high density diskette creating 8 sectors/track and will reserve the room for system files.
    c) It will format a 360 KB disk of 3.5" or 5.25" and will make the disk bootable,

d)   It will format a 360 KB disk creating 8 sectors/ track.

6.   DELTREE command can delete -

a)   All the files within the directories and sub-directories.

b)   All the files and sub-directories in a directory.

c)   All the sub-directories and will copy the file from sub-directories to parent directory.

d)   None of these.

7.   PROMPT $P$$ will change the prompt to

a)   C:\$ b)   C:\(Current date)

c)   C:\<d)C:$>

8.   While creating the file from COPY CON command last character must be

a)   Ctrl+Z   b)   Ctrl+C

c)   Ctrl+F6   d)   Any of above.

9.   MOVE command is equivalent to

a)   DEL Command

b)   COPY command

c)   COPY & DEL command

d)   None of these.

TRUE & FALSE :

10.   Literal stands for one or more character where as wild card stands for a single character.

11.   The label of disk can be changed with LABEL command.

12.   DOS can accept any date between year 1909 and 2099.

13.   CHKDSK can also fix error on disk.

14.   Root directory is the last level in multilevel directory.

15.   TREE command displays the structure of directory in a tabular manner.

16. With the help of COPY command, duplicate copy of files can be created with same name.

16. With COPY command, sub-directories with all its files can be copied.

17. CD command will display the present working directory.

18. PATH command directs the DOS to search the executable files in the specified sub-directories along with the current directory.

19. COPY A.TXT + B.TXT will copy both files in A.TXT.

20. DEL command can also erase sub-directories.

21. REN command is not applicable to directories.

22. RD command can be used to delete the entire sub-directory and its files.

23. Data can be stored on a newly purchased disk.

24. Wild cards are * and #.

SHORT ANSWER QUESTIONS

25. Distinguish between external and internal commands. Explain with example.

26. Specify whether the following commands are external command or internal command : (If external, also name the file associated)

    - COPY   - DIR
    - DELTREE   - DATE
    - DISKCOPY   - LABEL
    - ERASE   - VOL
    - MD   - TREE
    - CD   - PATH
    - SYS   - REN

27. Write the commands to accomplish following task -

    - Copy all the files with extension .EXE from C drive to B Drive.

- Rename all the files with secondary name .COM on the disk A as .EXE files.
- Change the date to 1st Jan.1980
- to make a directory HILTRON on A Drive.
- Make a sub-directory CALC inside HILTRON on A.
- Copy all files from C root to CALC in A drive.
- To transfer the system files to floppy disk A.

PIPE, REDIRECTION AND DOS FILTERS
STORING SCREEN OUTPUT ON DISKFILE
PROCESSING YOUR FILE INFORMATION
DOS OPERATION AND PIPES

Pipe, Redirection and DOS Filters

The redirections and pipes are quite useful and fascinating functions of DOS. These features are interrelated to each other. Basically redirection enables you to act like a railway engineer, switching trains from one track to another. Here DOS command's output can be considered as train, and redirections & pipes gives us the ability to send it to the required place.

Redirection : It refers to the ability of a program or DOS command to choose new alternative device or file for input or output. Most programs of DOS have a default device like in DIR Command, the computer assumes that you want a directory to be displayed on the screen.

The other output devices to which the information can be sent are :

- Printer
- Diskfile

You can define the other device or file to be command's output destination by preceding the device or file name with the >symbol. Similarly a device or file can be assigned as command's input by preceding the device or filename with <Symbol.

STORING SCREEN OUTPUT ON DISKFILE

To send the output of a DOS command to a disk file, use the following command

Syntax

DOS Command > (filename)

When the above command is executed at DOS prompt, the information which is to be displayed on the screen, is transferred to the given file name and no visible result is produced on the screen.

To check the result you can view the contents of the file by giving TYPE Command.

E.g.DIR A: >CATALOG

The above command with redirect the output i.e. directory of A to a file named CATALOG rather than displaying it on the screen.

TYPE CATALOG will display the contents of CATALOG file which is just the duplicate of the DIR Command output. But if you add or delete files on the A:drive, the CATALOG file will not reflect any changes.

ADDING OUTPUT TO AN EXISTING FILE

The redirected output can also be added at the end of existing file. For that the command is :

Syntax

DOS Command > (filename)

Here the first command simply replaces the old file with a new one. The second command causes the output from the present DOS command to be appended to (added to the end of) the existing file.

E.g.DIR B: >CATALOG
DIR A:>> CATALOG

The first command will redirect the directory of B to CATALOG file on the default drive. The second command will append the directory of A to the same file.

SENDING OUTPUT TO THE PRINTER

To obtain a hardcopy printout of the information that appears on the screen, you can press Shift & PrtScr keys simultaneously. But that will send only one screenful of information to the printer.

To send the complete output of any DOS Command to the printer, DOS has a simple way of redirecting the output. Including > PRN with the DOS command will redirect the output of any DOS command to the printer, no matter how many screenful of information of data are involved.

Syntax

DOS Command > PRN.

E.g. DIR > PRN

CHKDSK > PRN

Again when the information is redirected to printer, no visible result is produced on the screen.

RECEIVING INPUT FROM TEXTFILE

DOS can also receive input from a textfile. This means that instead of waiting to enter data, make responses, you can type your responses in advance. DOS will then take each response from the input file as it is needed.

Syntax

DOS Command < (filename)

PROCESSING YOUR FILE INFORMATION

Another powerful feature of DOS is its use of filters to process data directly. A DOS filter can process in unique way any data that passes through it and can change what you seem the screen. There are three filters in DOS

- SORT
- FIND
- MORE.

All three are external commands and are stored on disk as SORT.EXE, FIND.EXE. and MORE.COM files.

SORT FILTER

SORT rearranges the data. It reads input, sorts data and writes the result to the screen, a file or another device. It acts as a filter, reading characters in a specified column and rearranging them in ascending or descending order.

Syntax

SORT [/R] [/+n] [<] [drive1:] [path1] file 1 [>[drive2:][path2] file2}

Parameters

[drive1:][path1] file1

> Specifies the location and name of the file whose data you want to sort.

[drive2:] [path2] file2

> Specifies the Location and name of a file in which the sorted output is to be stored.

/R

> Reverses the order of the sorting operation; i.e. sorts from Z to A and then from 9 to 0.

/+n

> Sorts the file according to the character in column n. If you do not use switch, the SORT command sorts data according to the characters in column1.

Let us assume that a text file Business.TXT contains the following data

NIRANJAN	GHAZIABAD	212/212/215/95
AMBICA	GHAZIABAD	213/210/221-96
ANU	BAREILLY	212/222/212-95
MANAV	JALANDHAR	202/222/202-95
RITA	DELHI	211/211/211-95

Using the redirection concept, you can sort the above list. Type the Command:

SORT < BUSINESS.TXT

This command will read the Business.Txt and will send the sorted output to the display screen.

AMBICA	GHAZIABAD	213/210/221-96
ANU	BAREILLY	212/222/212-95
MANAV	JALANDHAR	202/222/202-95
NIRANJAN	GHAZIABAD	212/212/215-95
RITA	DELHI	211/211/211-95

Here the sorting has taken place on the alphabets in Col.No.1.

If we want the sorting at some other column then include the column number in the sort command.

SORT < Business.TXT/+20

Here the sorting takes place on the 20th column character. Here the standard output result appears on the video display unit, since no redirection was specified for output. To redirect the above output to some other file or to printer, type the following command :

SORT <Business.TXT >CLIENTS.TXT

The command SORT is being directed to take its input from the < file and send its output to the > file.

FIND FILTER

It searches for a specific string of text in a file. After searching the specified files, FIND displays all lines of text that contains the specified string.

Syntax

FIND [/V] [/C] [/N] [/I] "String" [(drive:) (path) filename (....)].

Parameters

"String"   Specifies the group of characters you want to search for. You must enclose the text String in quotation marks.

[drive:][path] filename

Specifies the location and name of the file, in which to search for the specified string.

Switches

/ V   Displays all lines not containing the specified string.

/C   Displays only a count of the lines that contains the specified string.

/N   Precedes each line with the file's line number.

/I   Specifies that the search is not be case sensitive.

E.g.FIND "212" BUSINESS.TXT

The command will locate all lines that contains the specified character string (the first parameter) in the specified textfile.

MORE FILTER

It causes the screen display to pause just as /P switch does with DIR Command. Since some DOS commands accept the /P switch to process data one screenful, More is only used with those DOS command that do not allow screenful processing.

Syntax

MORE < [drive:] [path] filename.

[drive:] [path] filename.

Specifies the location and name of a file that supplies data you want to display.

E.g.   MORE < REPORT.TXT.

display one screenful of information of REPORT.TXT at a time.

DOS OPERATION AND PIPES

The filters till now are used only with files. When the filter work in connection with other programs or DOS Commands, the filters are called pipes. Pipes allows you to combine the power of redirection along with filter. You can simultaneously change your data while it is being moved (redirected) from one Location to another. The pipes are shown by | symbol.

Syntax

Output | filter

Here the output can be that of a standard DOS Command or from the textfile. The filter is applied to that output only.

E.g.   DIR | SORT

here the standard output would have been the directory of default drive, but when combined with filter SORT, it displays the directory of default drive in sorted order.

SOME MORE EXAMPLE ON PIPES, FILTERS & REDIRECTION

SORT/HO <File1> File2

-       It changes the contents of file 1, on the basis of 10th column and sends the output to file2.

DIR |SORT >PRN

-       redirects the sorted directory to the selected printer.

DIR | FIND d/n"<DIR>" >ABC.TXT

-       Takes the input from DIR Command, and searches all the lines for "<DIR>" strings. The lines, containing the strings, along with the liner number are redirected to a file ABC.TXT.

SUMMARY

REDIRECTION

Alternative signs can be chosen for input or output. > symbol is used for output and < symbol for input.

DOS Command > filename

-       sends the output to a non existing file.

DOS Command >> file name

-       adds the output to an existing file.

DOS Command > PRN

-       sends the output to printer.

DOS Command < (filename)

-       Accepts the input from a file.

SORT < input >output

-       Accepts the input, sort the input and send the sorted output to defined output.

FIND "string"

-       Searches for a specific string of text in a file.

MORE <input

-       causes the screen display to pause for the defined input.

PIPES

-       when filter works in connection with other DOS commands it is called pipe. Shown by (|) Symbol.

Output | filter

-       send the output through filter.

EXERCISE

TRUE OR FALSE:

1.   The V D U is the standard output unit for all Dos commands

2.   The output can be redirected to printer and file.

3.   Dos can't recieve the input from a text file.

4.   All the Dos filters are extenal commands.

5.   Sort/R will display the result in reverse order.

6.   Number of occurance of a particuler string can't be counted with the help of find command.

7.   Filters when used with files are called pipes.

8.   The output of a Dos command can be added in the middle of an existing text file.

9.   SORT<CALC.TXT/+20 mile take the input from CALC.TXT and will display the file sorted at 20th column.

10.   If not specified, sorting is case senstive.

11.   >> symbol is used to add the output of a Dos command to exiting text file.

SHORT ANSWER QUESTIONS:

12.   Write down the purpose of following commands:

   a) DIR A:> BUSINESS.TXT

   b) DIR B: | SORT >> BUSINESS.TXT.

   c) SORT/R/+10<TEXT.TXT >CALC.TXT

   d) SORT/R<B:\CALC\ HILL.DBF>>PRN

   e) FIND/C "HILTRON" B:\CALC\HILL.DBF

   f) MORE < C:\HILL.DBF

   g) FIND/ I/N " HILTRON" B:\CALC.TXT>HILL.TXT

   h) CHKDSK> ABC.TXT

   i) TYPE HILL.DBF | MORE

   j) TYPE HILL.DBF | MORE>>ABC.TXT

13. Distinguish between Filter and Pipes. Give one example of each.

ADVANCE DOS COMMANDS

Advance DOS Commands

MSBACKUP COMMAND

Backup for MS-DOS 6.0 and higher version is menu driven and makes it easy to use. Backup starts from DOS prompt by typing MSBACKUP and pressing Enter.

It backs up or restores one or more files from one disk onto another. You can backup all files on a disk or files that have changed since your last backup, Schedule backups so they are done automatically on a regular basis and restores files that you have backed up.

Syntax

MSBACKUP [Setup-files]

Setup-files specifies files to backup and the type of backup you want to perform. MSBACKUP creates a setup file when you save program settings and file selections. Setup files must have an SET extension. If you don't specify a setup file, MSBACKUP uses DEFAULT.SET.

When you run the MSBACKUP for the first time, you are prompted to perform a compatibility test. It ensures that BACKUP is set properly for your Computer.

After the compatibility test, you can configure your VDU and mouse if you wish to use one with backup.

After configuring, it displays a screen, from where you can pick the different operations, simply pick the Backup, Compare, Restore, or options. A corresponding screen is displayed.

BACKING UP FILES

From main Backup Screen, pick the files button to display a directory tree. You can pick drives, directories and files here. You can include or exclude the files and directories for backing up.

Once you select driver, directories and files, pick the start button to begin the backup operation.

BACKUP TYPE

When backing up files, you can perform different levels of backup by picking one of the following backup types in the backup type selection box.

Full backup   Backs up all files on your hard drive. It takes longer as compared to other types.

Incremental backup   Backs up those files that have changed since the last time a backup was performed. This is a fast backup method.

Differential backup It backup those files that have changed since the last time a backup was performed. It records the latest version of the file.

RESTORING FILE

To Restore files, select the Restore option from main menu and select drives, directories and files, pick the start button.

COMPARING FILES

It compares backup files to the source files to ensure the integrity of the backup. Use the compare screen's select files button to compare specific drives, directories or files. Use the option button, to display available options.

RESTORE COMMAND

It restores files that were backed up by using any version of BACKUP from MS-DOS version 2.0 to 5.0. The restoring can be done from similar or dissimilar disk types.

Restores files that were backed up by using any version of BACKUP from MS-DOS versions 2.0 through 5.0. If you are restoring files that were backed up using the MSBACKUP command in MS-DOS 6, use the <MSBACKUP> program to restore files.

You can restore files from similar or dissimilar disk types.

Syntax

RESTORE drive1:drive2:[path(filename)] [/S] [/P] [/B:date] [/A:date] /[E:time] [/L:time] [/M] [/N] [/D]

Parameters

drive1:   specifies the drive on which the backed-up files are stored.

drive2:   specifies the drive to which the backed-up files will be restored.

path :   specifies the directory to which the backed-up files will be restored. You must specify the same directory from which the files were backed up.

Filename :   specifies the names of the backed-up files you want to restore.

Switches

/S   Restores all sub-directories.

/P   Prompts you for permission to restore files that are read-only (that have the read-only attribute set) or that have changed since the last backup (that have the archive attribute set).

/B:date   Restores only those files last modified on or before the specified date. The format of date varies according to the COUNTRY setting in your CONFIG.SYS file. For information about specifying date, see the <DATE> command.

/A:date	Restores only those files last modified on or after the specified date. The format of date varies according to the COUNTRY setting in your CONFIG.SYS file. For information about specifying date, see the <DATE> command.
/E:time	Restores only those files last modified at or earlier than the specified time. The format of time varies according to the COUNTRY setting in your CONFIG.SYS file. For information about specifying time, see the ,TIME> command.
/L:time	Restores only those files last modified at or later than the specified time. The format of time varies according to the COUNTRY setting in your CONFIG.SYS file. For information about specifying time, see the <TIME> command.
/M	Restores only those files modified since the last backup.
/N	Restores only those files that no longer exist on the destination disk.
/D	Displays a list of the files on the backup disk that match the names specified in filename without restoring any files. Even though no files are being restored, you must specify drive2 when you use /D.

ATTRIB COMMAND

It is used to change the attribute of a file. This command displays, sets, or removes the Read-only, Archive, System, and Hidden attributes assigned to files or directories.

Syntax

ATTRIB (+R|-R) (+A|-A) (+S|-S) (+H|-H) [(drive:) (path) filename] [/S]

To display all attributes of all files in the current directory, use the following Syntax :

ATTRIB

Parameter

[drive:] [path] filename

> specifies the location and name of the file(s) you want to process.

Switches

+R	Sets the Read-only file attributes.
- R	Clean the Read-only file attributes.
+A	Sets the Archive file attribute.
- A	Clears the Archive file attribute.
+S	Sets the file as a system file.
- S	Clears the file as a system file.
+H	Sets the file as a Hidden file.
- H	Clears the hidden file attributes.
/S	Processes files in the current directory and all its sub-directories.

E.g.   ATTRIB +R CHKDSK.COM

The above command makes the CHKDSK program read only.

ATTRIB +H COMMAND.COM

Makes the COMMAND.COM as hidden file. The file doesn't appear when DIR command is given.

XCOPY COMMAND

It is used to selectively COPY files from one disk to another or those files that have been created or modified since the last backup with this command you can copy all the files in a directory, including the files in the sub-directory of the directory.

Syntax

XCOPY Source [destination] [/Y|/-Y] [/A|/M][/D|date] [/ P] [/S] [/E] [/V] [/W]

Parameters

Source: specifies the location and names of the files you want to copy. Source must include either a drive or a path.

Destination:Specifies the destination of the files you want to copy. Destination can include a drive letter and colon, a directory name, a filename, or a combination.

Switches

/Y indicates that you want XCOPY to replace existing file(s) without prompting you for confirmation. By default, if you specify an existing file as the destination file,

XCOPY will ask you if you want to overwrite the existing file. (Previous versions of MS-DOS would simply replace the existing file.) If the XCOPY command is part of a batch file, XCOPY will behave as in previous versions. Specifying this switch overrides all defaults and the current setting of the COPYCMD environment variable.

/-Y indicates that you want XCOPY to prompt you for confirmation when replacing an existing file. Specifying this switch overrides all defaults and the current setting of the COPYCMD environment variable.

/A copies only source files that have their archive file attributes set. This switch does not modify the archive file attribute of the source file. For

	information about how to set the archive file attribute, see the ATTRIB command.
/M	copies source files that have their archive file attributes set. Unlike the /A switch, the /M switch turns off archive file attributes in the files specified in source. For information about how to set the archive file attribute, see the <ATTRIB> command.
/D:date	copies only source files modified on or after the specified date. Note that the format of date depends on the COUNTRY setting you are using.
/P	Prompts you to confirm whether you want to create each destination file.
/S	Copies directories and sub-directories, unless they are empty. If you omit this switch, XCOPY works within a single directory.
/E	Copies any sub-directories, even if they are empty.
/V	Verifies each file as it is written to the destination file to make sure that the destination files are identical to the source files.
/W	Displays the following message and waits for your response before starting to copy files *Press any key to begin copying file(s)*.

E.g.   XCOPY C:\ E:\ /s

Copies all files from C:drive to E:drive including all files in the subordinate directories paths.

XCOPY C:\WP E:\ /S /P

Copies all files from C:\WP path to E:\WP file path. Any file path that are subordinate to \WP are also copies from drive

C to drive E. It also prompts a y/N ? option before copying a file.

MODE COMMAND

It configures system devices. The MODE Command performs many different tasks, such as displaying system status, changing system settings etc.

Traditional use of MODE Command is to control the output on the screen. ON display unit mode command can control several output including :

- Width (40 or 80 characters)
- Monochrome or Colour
- Specify the number of Lines and Columns.

Examples :

MODE 40   Displays 40 character per line.

MODE 80   Displays 80 characters per line.

MODE BW40   Displays 40 characters per line in monochrome.

MODE BW80   Displays 80 characters per line in monochrome.

MODE CO40   Displays 40 column per line in color.

MODE CO80   Displays 80 columns per line in color.

MODE MONO   Switches display output to the monochrome board or mode.

To specify the number of display lines and columns, the general command is :

MODE CON COLS = m LINES = n

Valid column values m are 40 and 80.

Valid line values n are 25,43 and 50.

The above command is valid only on EGA (Enhanced Graphic) and VGA (Video Graphic) Display.

REQUIREMENT OF ANSI.SYS AND DISPLAY.SYS

MODE Can perform some tasks, such as setting the display mode, only if you have included a DEVICE command for the ANSI.SYS device driver in your CONFIG.SYS file.

DOSKEY COMMAND

It loads the DOSKEY Program into memory. The DOSKEY program recalls MS-DOS Commands and enables you to edit command lines and create and run macros.

DOSKEY is a memory resident program. When installed, it occupies about 3 kilobytes of memory. To start DOSKEY Program use the following Syntax :

DOSKEY

FDISK COMMAND

FDISK is a menu driven program that sets up partition on your hard disk. You can review current partition information, delete old partitions and add new ones. A single partition may hold upto 2 gigabytes of data.

Syntax

FDISK

To display partition information without starting the FDISK program, use the following syntax :

FDISK /STATUS

Switch

/STATUS   Displays an overview of the partition information of your computer's hard disk(s), without starting the FDISK program.

Before your hard disk can be formatted to accept data, it must be portioned. This command is generally not needed in everyday use. Deleting a partition permanently deletes all the data stored on that partition.

REPLACE COMMAND

It selectively updates files on a target directory by replacing them with files of the same name on a source directory or adds files to the target directory from the source.

Syntax

REPLACE [drive1:][path1] filename [drive2:] [path2] [/A] [/P] [/R] [/W]

REPLACE [drive1:] [path1] filename [drive2:] [path2] [/P] [/R] [/S] [/W] [/U]

Parameters

[drive1:] [path1] filename

> Specifies the location and name of the source file or set of files.

[drive2:] [path2]

> Specifies the location of the destination file. You cannot specify a filename for files you replace. If you specify neither a drive nor a directory, REPLACE uses the current drive and directory as the destination.

Switches

/A   Adds new files to the destination directory instead of replacing existing files. You cannot use this switch with the /S or /U switch.

/P   Prompts you for confirmation before replacing a destination file or adding a source file.

/R   Replaces read-only files as well as unprotected files. If you do not specify this switch but attempt to replace a read-only file, an error results and stops the replacement operation.

/S   Searches all sub-directories of the destination directory and replaces matching files. You cannot use the /S switch with the /A switch. The REPLACE command does not search sub-directories specified in path1.

/W   Waits for you to insert a disk before REPLACE begins to search for source files. If you do not specify /W, REPLACE begins replacing or adding files immediately after you press ENTER.

/U   Replaces (updates) only those files on the destination directory that are older than those in the source directory. You cannot use the /U switch with the /A switch.

Replace differs from the COPY command in that it is more flexible, allowing various optional approaches to the process of copying files from one location to another.

UNDELETE COMMAND

It recovers accidentally deleted files.

Syntax

UNDELETE[(drive:) (path) filename] [/DOS]

UNDELETE [/LIST|/ALL (drive) |/STATUS|/LOAD|/UNLOAD

|/S [drive] |/Tdrive[/Entries)]

For best results, invoke UNDELETE before any other information is written to the disk. Subsequent disk writes may overwrite the disk area occupied by deleted file, making recovery impossible.

UNDELETE displays each deleted file it finds that matches the specification in Command line. It prompts you to re-enter the first character in the filename, which was lost when file was deleted. After you enter the characters, UNDELETE attempts to recover the file.

Parameter

[drive:] [path] filename

> Specifies the location and name of the file or set of files you want to recover. By default, UNDELETE restores all deleted files in the current directory.

Switches

/LIST

> Lists the deleted files that are available to be recovered, but does not recover any files.The [drive:] [path] filename parameter and the /DT, /DS, and /DOS switches control the listing produced by this switch.

/ALL

> Recovers deleted files without prompting for confirmation on each file.
>
> UNDELETE recovers files from the DOS directory, supplying a number sign (#) for the missing first character in the filename. If a duplicate filename already exists, this switch next tries each of the following characters, in the order listed, until the result is a unique filename:
>
> **#%&0123456789ABCDEFGHIJKLMNOPQRSTUVWXYZ.**

/DOS

> Recovers only those files that are internally listed as deleted by MS/DOS, prompting for confirmation on each file. If a deletion-tracking file exists, this switch causes UNDELETE to ignore it.

/LOAD

> Loads the UNDELETE memory-resident program into memory using information defined in the UNDELETE.INI file. If the UNDELETE.INI file does not exist, UNDELETE uses default values.

/UNLOAD

> Unloads the memory-resident portion of the UNDELETE program from memory, turning off the capability to restore deleted files.

/STATUS   Displays the type of delete protection in effect for each drive.

/S[drive] | Disk Size Entries | File Size |
|---|---|
| 360K | 355K |
| 720 K | 509K |
| 1.2 MB | 7514K |
| 1.44MB | 7514K |
| 20 MB | 10118K |
| 32 MB | 20236K |
| 32 MB | 30355K |

VERIFY COMMAND

Directs MS-DOS to verify that your files are written correctly to a disk and displays the status of verification. For example, you can use this command to make sure data is not written to a bad sector. You can use this command either at the command prompt or in your AUTOEXEC.BAT file.

Syntax

VERIFY [ON|OFF]

Switch

ON/OFF   Specifies whether MS-DOS should verify (ON) or not verify (OFF) that write operations are done correctly.

SUMMARY

MSBACKUP	backup or restores one or more files from one disk onto another.
RESTORE	restores files that were backed up by using any version of BACKUP from
MSDOS	versions 2.0 through 5.0.
ATTRIB	used to change the attribute of a file.
XCOPY	used to selectively copy files from one disk to another.
MODE	configures system devices.
DOSKEY	It loads the DOSKEY program into memory.
FDISK	sets up partition on your hard disk.
REPLACE	Selectively updates files on a target directory by replacing them.
UNDELETE	recovers accidentally deleted files.
VERIFY	directs MS-DOS to verify that your files are written correctly to a disk and displays the status of verification.

EXERCISE

TRUE OR FALSE

1. MSBACKUP is a menu driven command and performs the functions of Backup, Restores & Compare.

2. Any file or directory can be made a hidden file using ATTRIB command.

3. FDISK command is used to create partition on the disk.

4. A single partition on disk can hold upto 4 gigabytes of data.

5. Maximum 80 lines can be displayed on the screen.

6. The deleted files can be displayed on the screen with UNDELETE command.

7. ANSI.SYS must be loaded through CONFIG.SYS if number of lines on the screen are to be changed.

8. Incremental Backup, backs up all files on your hard disk.

OBJECTIVE TYPE QUESTIONS

9. What does UNDELETE/ALL do?

    a) Undelete all files after prompting.

    b) Undelete all files without prompting.

    c) None of the above.

10. What is the significance of /D switch in the restore command?

    a) Deletes the source after restoring to the target.

    b) Restores files matching to the data specified.

    c) Display files on disk that matches specification.

    d) None of the above.

11. What does the command VERIFY ON do?

    a) Verify the disk after format.

    b) Verifies the disk to see that there are no bad sectors present.

ADVANCED DOS COMMANDS

c) Makes DOS to check whether data was written correctly to the disk.

12. The /e switch of XCOPY command

 a) Copies source file modified on or time specified.

 b) Copies subdirectories even if they are empty.

 c) Error message "Empty subdirectories Ignore Y/N".

 d) Makes a Xerox copy of an erased file in same subdirectory.

13. To selectively add or replace files on a disk so that you can update the destination disk with more recent version of files from the source disk, the command you would use is,

 a) RESTORE b) REPLACE

 c) COPY d) DELETE & COPY

14. What does the /S switch of the REPLACE command signify?

 a) Searches all sub-directories of the destination directory for a match with the source file.

 b) Allows you to specify selective source files to replace.

 c) None of the above.

15. The RESTORE command of DOS

 a) Restores files backed-up by the BACKUP command.

 b) Replaces files which are corrupt.

 c) Restores the dameged disk.

 d) None of the above.

16. What does the /b switch of the RESTORE command signify?

 a) Restores only binary format.

 b) Restores files modified on or before date specified.

 c) Restores files backwards.

 d) Restores ASCII files backward.

FILE EXECUTION & BATCH FILES

File Execution & Batch Files

The hard disk or floppy drive have many files, directories and sub-directory in it. If some command is given at DOS prompt and it performs the specific purpose, it is called that it is being executed.

The DOS has two type of commands, Internal & External and the Internal commands requires the basic file IO.SYS, MSDOS.SYS & COMMAND.COM. for execution, where as External commands requires the special programs along with the above three files.

If you go through all the external DOS command, in the directory of DOS, you will find one or more file for each command. You can also note that for each of the external command there exist a file with the command name and .EXE [executable] or COM [command] as extension name. In fact these are the main files which let the DOS command run from DOS prompt.

In fact all the external files and programs having .EXE. or .COM extension, are executable at DOS prompt. There are precompiled files and can't be created by user. (Even if the user create a file with EXE extension, it is of no meaning).

The only files, which user can create and are executable at DOS prompt, are Batch files with .BAT extension.

CONCEPT OF BATCHFILE

Till now the discussions has been made about the DOS commands and their usage. To use a DOS command, it is required to type in the command at prompt. When command is complete, the DOS displays the prompt again, which indicates that DOS is ready for another command.

Batch file allows you to enter a group of DOS commands automatically. A batch file is a series of ordinary DOS commands that the computer can execute automatically as a group (a batch) instead of one at a time.

GUIDELINES FOR BATCH FILE

- Each batch file should be a completely ASCII file with .BAT filename extension. It can be created by using the COPY CON command at DOS prompt or DOS editor EDIT.

- Each command line should end with a carriage return and line feed pair of characters.

- Choose a filename upto eight characters, but be careful not to use a name already used by DOS Command's names.

RUNNING AND STOPPING BATCH FILES

To execute all the instructions within a batch file, simply type the name of .BAT program containing the instruction. It takes the default drive if no drive name is specified.

To stop batch file execution at any time press, Ctrl+pause combination from the key board. DOS will display ^C and will ask you if you want to terminate the batch job. Usually you enter Y for yes and N for no. If you press N, current step is the batch file will be ignored and rest of the commands will be executed.

Example

C>COPYCON ABC.BAT

PROMPT PQ

DATE 04-01-1995

TIME 12:00:00.35

Ver

Vol

LABEL HILTRON

^Z

^Z saves the files into your default drive. Now in the above batch file, few DOS commands has been given. When the batch file is execute, the commands are displayed at the screen one by one and executed. For executing the batch file simply write the batch file name ABC at DOS prompt.

REPLACEABLE PARAMETERS

Many useful batch files do nothing more than slavishly execute the same series of commands each time they run. This is a perfectly acceptable use of batch files, but it carries a drawback. You must write a new batch file for any variation in parameters of command.

DOS allows you a greater degree of flexibility by permitting you to include upto 9 parameters on the command line when you invoke the batch file. These command line parameters are referenced in the batch file using percent sign (%) followed by number 1 through 9.

Let us consider a simple batch file FINISH.BAT.

DEL C:\COBOL*.BAK.

DIR C:\COBOL > PRN.

The above batch file when executed deletes all .BAK files from COBOL directory and then send the directory of COBOL sub-directory to printer.

The above file is rigid in nature as it will be able to deal with COBOL sub-directory only. Suppose it is required to run the file for some other directory then modifications are required in this file.

But if we include replaceable parameters in FINISH.BAT, we can repeat the same act for different sub-directories.

DEL C:%1 *.BAK.

DIR C:%1 >%2

Having place %1 and %2 in the batch file you can supply the variable directory name and output device name while invoking the FINISH batch file.

E.g.To delete all *.BAK files from COBOL directory and send the output to printer the command will be

FINISH \COBOL PRN

Similarly to delete all .BAK files from PROJECT sub-directory and send the output to a file PRO.TXT the command will be

FINISH \PROJECT PRO.TXT

Although use of this technique means that you must enter an additional parameter on the command line, you have gained flexibility for your batch file, as it can be used on any directory path in your system, including nested sub-directories.

If you enter nothing along with batch file name at prompt, DOS would replace the parameters with nothing and will execute the commands accordingly.

e.g.   DEL C:*.BAK
**   DIR C:>**

Batch files have their own set of specialized support commands known as subcommands. Depending on what type of batch program you write, you may need to use one or several sub-commands.

The following is the list of specially designed batch sub commands :

<CALL><If
<ECHO><Pause>
<GOTO><Rem>
<@><:>
<FOR><CHOICE>

You can use the command /Y to step through a batch program line by line, and can selectively by pass or carry out individual command.

CHAINING BATCH FILE

Batch files can run programs or other batch file. However, there is a difference between chaining batch files and calling other batchfile.

When we call a batch file, it indicates that we want to run the original batch file but want to insert the other batch file in it. But when we chain two batch file, it indicates that after complete execution of batch file we are transferring the control to other batch file.

To invoke the next batch file after execution of first simply type the name of other batch file in end of present batch file.

Consider two batch file. FIRST.BAT and .SECOND.BAT.

REM FIRST. BAT
DEL C:\COBOL*.BAK
DEL C:\COBOL*.OBI
ECHO. Transfer the Control to SECOND
SECOND
REM SECOND.BAT
DEL C:\COBOL*.IDX
COPY C:\COBOL*.*A:

Here in the above example after the FIRST.BAT is executed, the control is transferred to SECOND.BAT. and after executing SECOND.BAT control is transferred to DOS prompt.

THE AUTOEXEC.BAT FILE

DOS makes use of one special batch file named AUTOEXEC.BAT. If this batch file exists on the root directory of the boot drive, the DOS commands in this file will execute automatically, whenever the computer is started up or rebooted. This batch file usually contains special configuration and start up DOS commands, but it may contain any valid DOS or application command you want.

Creating AUTOEXEC.BAT is similar to creating any other batch file.

C> COPY CON AUTOEXEC.BAT

@ ECHO OFF

ECHO HELLO FRIENDS, WELCOME TO HILTRON-CALC

^Z

So each time you switch on the computer, the above batch file will display the message "HELLO........". This file must exist at the root of DOS disk otherwise it will not get executed.

ECHO COMMAND

It suppresses or displays batch file lines on the screen.

Syntax

ECHO ON/OFFMessage

The purpose of Echo command is :

-      Not to display the unwanted commands on the screen.
-      to display custom message on the screen.

If you invoke ECHO ON, DOS will display each subsequent line on the screen as it is executed.

If you invoke ECHO with any other string character. DOS will display the message on the screen, regardless of whether ECHO has been set ON or OFF.

Ex.   **@ECHO OFF.**

         ECHO Deleting BAK files from Directory.............

DEL C:\%|\ *.BAK.

displays the message "Deleting BAK files from Directory...................." before command line is executed.

PAUSE COMMAND

When a batch file is being executed, at times it is required to interrupt the execution. This can be done by using the PAUSE Command.

When the PAUSE Command is encountered, the execution of the batch file stops and the following message is displayed on the screen :

Press any key to continue...................

of the user presses a key, the batch continue.

Syntax

PAUSE Message

Message parameter may be any string. How ever the message appears on the screen, only if ECHO is set ON and will include the PAUSE command itself.

@ ECHO OFF

CLS.

ECHO will delete BAK files in Directory

PAUSE

DEL C:%1*.BAK

REM COMMAND

Indicates that line is non-executable string, used to place explanatory remark within the batch file.

Syntax

REM String

It allows you to include remark in the file that explain what the file is doing. These remarks are helpful to others who read file or to yourself if you return to edit a file after a gap.

@ COMMAND

Suppresses the display of the line on the screen.

Syntax

@ Command

Command lives that include the @ Symbol are processed normally but are not displayed. This symbol must be the first character in the line.

Ex.@ECHO OFF

DEL C:\COBOL*.BAK

Here @ suppresses the display of ECHO OFF Command and ECHO OFF will prevent the display of subsequent commands.

IF COMMAND

The batch command IF is used to allow conditional execution of the commands. If the condition is true, executes a command, otherwise, ignores the command.

Syntax

To test a logical condition.

IF condition command

IF NOT condition command

To test for the existence of a file

IF EXIST file(s) command

IF NOT EXIST file(s) command

The condition parameter takes the form of a quality test, which compares two strings on the command line using two equal signs (==).

E.g. **IF "%1" == "/A" command**

Tests to see if the first parameter on the command line is /
A, If it is, the condition is evaluated as true and the command
following the condition is executed.

If the parameter is anything other than /A, the condition is
false and command is ignored.

The strings that are compared in equality test are care-
sensitive. Thus in above example /A wouldn't be equal to /
a.

IF EXIST C:%|\ *.BAK DEL C:%|*>BAK.

The above command deletes the .BAK file only when the
files are existing in the opted sub-directory.

If commands can be nested on the same line.

**e.g. IF NOT EXIST *.BAK IF NOT EXIST *.OLD ECHO "Not
Found"**

the above command test for the existence of files with a
.BAK extension. If none are found, then it tests for files with
an .OLD extension. If none are found, it displays the message
"Not found". If files of either types are found, the message
will not be displayed.

: (COLON)

Indicates a section label in a batch file for use by the GOTO
Command

Syntax

:(Label name)

In general, the legal characters for Label names are the
same as - the legal characters for DOS file names, the one
exception being that the period (.) is not used. Labels allow
DOS to jump to any line in a batch file, using the GOTO

command to reference a label positioned just before the target line.

GOTO COMMAND

Commands in a batch file are executed in sequence. However, the branch file can be made to branch off to a specific point, to execute a group of commands statements beginning at that point. The GOTO Command can be used to do this.

Syntax

GOTO Label

E.g.   @ ECHO OFF
        IF NOT EXIST C:%1 *.BAK GOTO SKIP
        DEL C:%1*.BAK
        ECHO Files deleted.
        GOTO ND
        : SKIP
        ECHO files not found
        GOTO END.
        :END

Here in the above example, the DOS first checks whether .BAK files exist in the defined directory or not.

If the files exist then it deletes the files display the message "Files deleted" and transfer the control to END label to stop the execution of batch file.

If the files doesn't exist, then DOS transfers the control to SKIP label, display the message "Files not found" and then again transfers the control to END Label to stop the execution of batch file.

CALL COMMAND

Invokes a second batch file from within a currently running batch file, then returns to the original batch file.

Syntax

CALL [drive:\path\] bath file

CALL requires the name of another batch file. The .BAT extension is not required. You may include a drive letter and directory path if not the currently logged one.

E.g. **@ ECHO OFF**

CALL WP

DEL C:\COBOL*.BAK

Here the batch file calls WP.BAT, executes it and then returns to the parent batch file to invoke the remaining commands.

FOR COMMAND

Allows DOS to execute a command repeatedly.

Syntax

FOR %%variable IN (dataset) DO command [%%variable]

The FOR command creates a condition called a loop, in which a single command is executed on a series of file parameters, untill all parameters in the series are exhausted. In the above syntax, dataset is the series of the parameters, %%variable is a symbol to be applied sequentially to each item in the data set and command is the DOS command to execute repeatedly, using each updated value for %%variable.

In other words, if this syntax were translated into plain English, it would read : " For each item in the indicated list, invoke the command, until you run out of items."

The IN and DO keyworks are required part of the FOR command. They must be positioned in the command line as shown.

E.g. **@ECHO OFF**

FOR %% X IN (*.BAK*.OLD)DO DEL %%%X

FOR %%x IN (*.*) DO IF NOT EXIST A:%%X COPY %%xA:

Deletes all the files with.BAK and .OLD extensions. Then, it copies each file in the current directory to drive A, if that file doesn't already exist on drive A. In other words, the second FOR loop copies only newly created files, skipping those that were copied previously.

CHOICE COMMAND

Prompts the user for a response and sets the ERRORLEVEL variable based on the response given.

Syntax

CHOICE/Switches prompt

The CHOICE command allows batch files to be interactive and allows you to write batch files that are more flexible and "intellligent", choosing between alternate processing based on user input. CHOICE displays a prompt and waits for the user to press a key in response. Switches give you the option of specifying which keys are valid responses and allowing an automatic default response if none is given after a specifid number of seconds.

The prompt parameter is a text string that the CHOICE command displays to the user. If you omit this parameter, CHOICE displays a default prompt based on the switches you have supplied.

Switches

/ C: Keys   Specifies the valid response keys, where keys is a character string representing the keys the user may press. When CHOICE pauses for input, these keys are displayed within brackets ([]), followed by a question mark. If you don't used this switch, valid response keys are Y and N.

/N   Suppresses display of the valid response keys.

/S   Forces response keys to be case sensitive. Upper and lowercase characters may be used in the /C keys switch. Default is non-case-sensitive (DOS accepts either upper-or lowercase characters).

/T.key,seconds

Pauses for the number of seconds specified by second, and if no response is given, accepts the character specified by key as the default response. The key parameter must be a key specified in the /C keys switch. The second parameter is a numbr in the range 0-99, if 0, CHOICE does not pause.

The following example displays a simple menu of options on the screen, and returns to the menu when each application is complete :

@ECHO OFF
:START
CLS
ECHO {W}ord Processor (WP.EXE)
ECHO {S}preadsheet (123.EXE)
ECHO {D}atabase (DBASE.EXE)
ECHO
CHOICE /C:WSDX/T:X,15 "CHOOSE AN APPLICATION, OR X
     TO EXIT"
IF ERRORLEVEL == 4 GOTO END
IF ERRORLEVEL == 3 GOTO DBASE
IF ERRORLEVEL == 2 GOTO LOTUS
IF ERRORLEVEL == 1 GOTO WP

```
:DBASE
DBASE
GOTO START
:LOTUS
123
GOTO START
:WP
WP
GOTO START
:END
```

SUMMARY

Batch File is a file consist of series of DOS commands that computer can execute automatically as a group instead of one at a time.

Batch file Commands

ECHO — suppresses or displays batch file lines on the screen.

PAUSE — Interrupts the execution of a batch file. Restarts when any key is pressed.

REM — places explanatory remarks in the batch file.

IF — used to allow conditional execution of commands.

: — indicates the para name, used with GOTO command in batch file.

GOTO — branches out the execution to execute a group of commands.

CALL — Invokes a second batch file within a currently running batch file.

AUTOEXEC.BAT — If this file exist on root, it is executed as soon as basic DOS files are loaded into memory.

EXERCISE

STATE TRUE OR FALSE

1.   Batch files are the files created by the user and are executable at DOS prompt.

2.   Batch file consist of series of command that are executed one by one, unattended.

3.   Ctrl+Break combination terminate the batch job without prompting the user.

4.   AUTOEXEC.BAT is executed automatically when computer is switched on.

5.   ECHO OFF command in the batch file supresses the display of command line on the screen.

6.   CALL command transfers the control from one batch file to another batch file and doesn't return the control to prevent batch file.

7.   During execution of Batch File, custom messages on the screen can be displayed by ECHO command.

8.   IF command in a batch file can't be nested.

OBJECTIVE TYPE QUESTIONS

9.   In a batch file, what does "@" symbol in front of a line signify?

    a)   REMARK

    b)   Mathematical function

    c)   Do not echo the command on user screen.

    d)   Do not echo all following lines on the screen.

10.   Suppose a batch file A.BAT contains the command DIR C:*.*. If at DOS prompt A>PRN is given, will the directory listing be redirected to the printer.

    a)   Yes   b)   No

11.   If a message is to be displayed on the screen the command is

    a)   TYPE <message>   b)   <message>

       c)   ECHO <message> d)   None of these

12. How many parameters are allowed in a batch file
   a) None   b) One
   c) Five   d) Nine

13. How can a batch file be terminated
   a) Not possible
   b) By pressing Ctrl+Break
   c) By pressing Ctrl+C and responding "Y" when asked for confirmation.
   d) None of the above.

14. What happens when you type "N" when asked for confirmation for terminating a batch process.
   a) DOS continues with the process as if it was not intrupted.
   b) DOS ends the command it is currently executing, continuing execution with the next command in the batch file.
   c) None of the above

15. What happens when DOS comes across the PAUSE command in a batch file?
   a) Pauses for a specified period and then continues.
   b) Returns an error message.
   c) Pauses and gives the following message
      Press any key to continue.......
   d) None of the above.

DOS EDITOR
THE DOS EDITOR
MOVING TEXT
THE SCREEN EDITOR-NE

DOS Editor

The DOS editor is line oriented word processor and is designed strictly for text files. It doesn't have word wrapping facility like other word processors. Therefore, when you get to end a line, you must press <Enter> to begin the next line.

THE DOS EDITOR

The editor is a self-contained program within DOS You can start editor from prompt by typing EDIT and pressing <Enter>. If you want to make changes to existing file type EDIT followed by file-name along with path.

Syntax

EDIT [(drive:) (path) filename]

This editor's main screen is shown in the fig. The screen has a bare of menus at the top, from which you can make selections and a status bar at the bottom. When working with Editor, you can use any of the cursor and scrolling keys as well as mouse.

They keys most often used to pull down menus and select options are given below.

EDITOR KEY	FUNCTION
Alt	To activate the menu bar
F1	To access on-line help.
F2	To switch between Help and Editing screens when the help screen is displayed.
Esc	To backout of the current window, menu or dialog box.

ADDING TEXT

The cursor is the small blinking underline that indicates where the next character you type will appear or the next change you make will take effect. You can position the cursor by clicking your mouse in the text or by using cursor movement keys.

To add text to a file, simply move the cursor where you want the text to begin and start typing. When you want to start a new line, move the cursor to the beginning or end of an existing line and press <Enter>..

Cursor movement keys used in DOS Editor

Function	Key
Character Left	←
Character Right	→
Word Left	^+←
Word Right	^+→
Line Up	↑
Line down	↓
Beginning of Line	Home
End of Line	End
Page Up	PgUp
Page down	PgDn

Beginning of File   Ctrl+Home

End Of File   Ctrl+End

MOVING TEXT

Suppose you want to move part of text from one place to another place. This process known as act-and-prate makes the things easier.

The first step is to select (block, or highlight) a portion of the text using the mouse or the keyboard. Here is how to select a block of text :

-    To select the text with mouse, place the mouse pointer at the beginning of the block that you want to select, then hold down the left mouse button while dragging the mouse to the end of the block. When all the text you want to select is highlighted, release the mouse button.

-    To select the text from keyboard, move the cursor to the beginning of the block, and then hold down the shift key while pressing the arrow keys or other cursor movement keys.

The next step is to choose Edit -> Cut or press shift + Del (the highlighted text will disappear) and then position the cursor to the place where you want to move the text. Finally choose Edit + Paste or press Shift + Ins. The selected Text will appear in its new location.

COPYING TEXT

Copying text also involves three steps, the first step being similar to the Moving text.

After selecting the text, choose Edit => Copy or press Ctrl + Ins. Now move the cursor to new text location and then choose Edit -> Paste or Shift + Ins.

DELETING TEXT

To delete a block of text, select the text, then choose Edit -> clear or press Del key. To delete a single character above the cursor, press the Del key. To delete a single character to the left of the cursor, press the Backspace key.

FINDING & REPLACING PHRASES

If your files in lengthy, you can let the Editor find or replace words so you don't have to make the changes manually. You can only search forward, so begin by placing the cursor in the text at the point where you want to begin searching.

If you want the Editor to find a word or phrase choose Search -> Find Enter the text in Find. What box and select the Match Upper/Lowercase and whose word options if you wish, and select OK. The Editor will find the first occurrence of the phrase. To continue searching, select Search -> Repeat last find or Press F3.

If you want the Editor to replace a word or phrase with another word or phrase choose Search - > change. Enter the original text in the Find what box and the replacement text in the change to box, specify the Match Upper/Lower case and whole word options (if you wish), then choose either change Alt (to change all occurrence without confirmation) or find And Verify (to change occurrences one by one). You also can use search - > change to delete a phrase by leaving the replacement text box empty.

SAVING A FILE

Once you've completed your changes, save them permanently. If you want to retain the same file name, simply select File - > Save. To save the file and rename it, select File - > Save As. If you wish, you can specify a new drive and directory for saved file.

PRINTING A FILE

To print the entire file, choose File -> Print. Alternatively you can print just part of the file by selecting the text you want to print, then choosing File -> Print.

EXITING THE EDITOR

To exit the Editor, simply select File -> exit. If you forget to save your file, you'll be prompted to save it before the Editor returns you to shell or command line.

THE SCREEN EDITOR-NE

Programmers using system probably spend most of their working lives using an editor than any other piece of software package. Writing programmes, preparing documents and test data, tabulation results are all done with the help of editor. Edlin-line editor suffers from major problem that it does not allow full cursor movement on screen, as it is a line editor. This problem becomes more serious while writing long programes as usually is the case with commercial programes. In order to overcome this problem, programers seek help of other editors. Norton Editor is one of the most widely used screen editor.

USING THE EDITOR - NE

NE is a text editor; an interactive program whose job is to allow you to create text file, manipulate text in a file, to move text, change it, add to it or delete it.

NE is invokved by typing NE at the DOS prompt. You can also give an argument if you like. The argument is the name of the file to be created/edited. In case, you simply type NE, you will get following display :

Enter File Name

Norton Editor

116

A programmers full screen editor

Version *.*

(C) Copywright * * * * * *

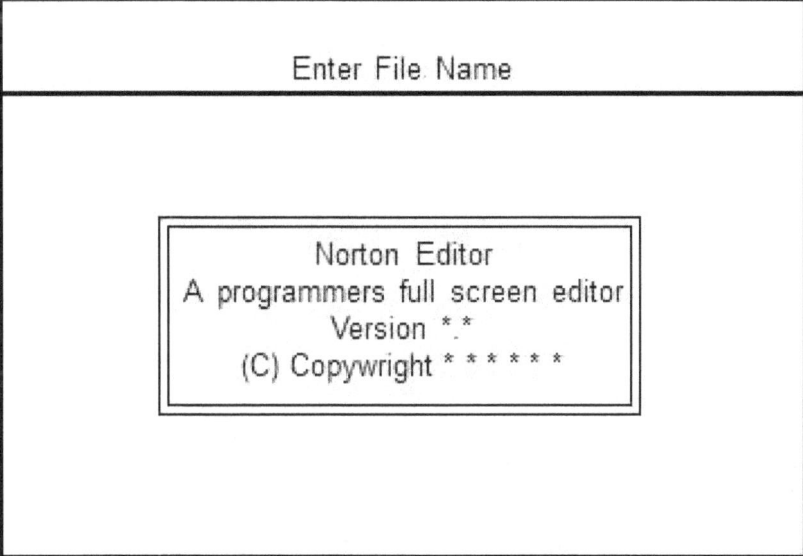

Fig.

Here you have to give file name which you want to create/ edit.

Whereas if you give NE with argument, then you will get directly screen display as shown in Fig.2

After this, when you press any key to start, you will get blank screen as shown in fig.3. NE has online help facility which you can use at any time by pressing F1 key without loosing anything.

Various controls and commands are listed in table 1 to 7. The same can be viewed by pressing F1 (Help key.)

CURSOR CONTROL COMMANDS

Keys	Function
←	Move cursor left
→	Move cursor right

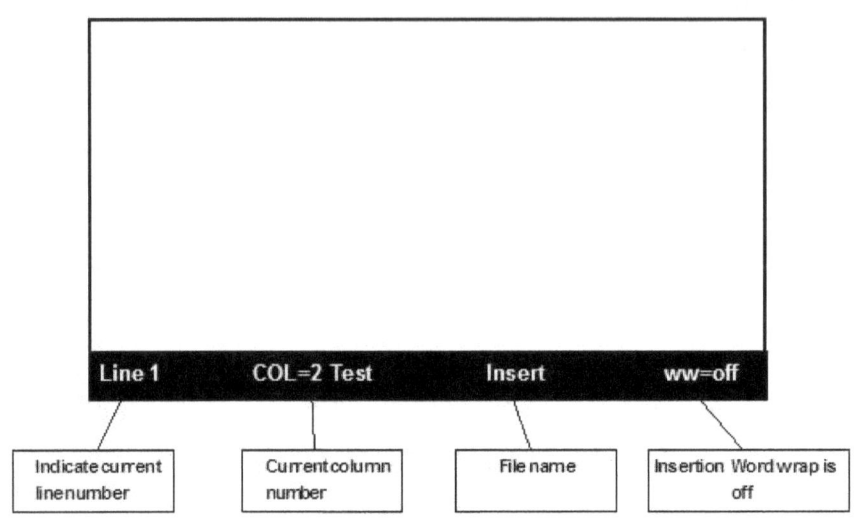

| Line 1 | COL=2 Test | Insert | ww=off |

| Indicate current line number | Current column number | File name | Insertion Wordwrap is off |

Fig

↑	Move cursor up
↓	Move cursor down
^←	Move cursor one word left
^→	Move cursor one word right
Home	Move to line beginning
End	Move to line end
PgUp	Move one page up
PgDn	Move one page down
Home	Move to file beginning
End	Move to the file end

Delete Commands

Backspace	Delete one character to the left of the cursor
Del	Delete one character to the right of the cursor
^+W	Delete one word left
Alt + W	Delete one word right
Control+L	Delete to line beginning
Alt+L	Delete to line end
Alt+K	Kill al characters on line
F4D	Delete a block

Control+U   Undelete text

File Commands

F3E	Save and exit
F3S	Save and don't exit
F3N	Edit a new file
F3X	Exchange windows
F3W	Write text to cursor
F3L	Load more of the file
F3	Append a file
F3C	Close the output file

Block Commands

F4S	Set a block market
F4R	Remove the markers
F4D	Delete a block
F4C	Copy a block
F4W	Copy block from wondiw
F4M	Move a block
F4L	Mark a line
F4E	Mark to line end
F4F	Find a block market

Screen Format Controls

F5L	Set line length for word wrap
F5W	Word Wrap toggle
F5F	Format a paragraph
F5T	Set tab display spacing
F5C	Select cursor type
F5D	Select display color
F5I	Induct toggle
F5S	Save editor configuration

Printer Commands

F7P	Print entire text buffer
F7B	Print a block

F7E	Eject printer page
F7S	Set page size for printing
F7M	Set left margin for printing

Additional Commands

F6 INS	Replace Mode
F9	DOS command Processor
F6 a	Go to line (by number)
ALT+F	Find string forward
Control+F	Find string reverse
Alt+C	Continue find string forward
Control+C	Continue find string reverse

Forward Search and Replace

Alt+F	Enter Search string
Ctrl+F	Enter replacement string.

Reverse Search and Replace

Control+F	Enter search string
Control+F	Enter replacement string.

APPENDIX A
COMMAND SUMMARY

ATTRIB Changes or disaplays the attributes of a file.

ATTRIB modes target drive:\path\file(s) /switches

CD or CHDIR Displays or changes the currently logged subdirectory.

CHDIR drive:\path

CHKDSK Analyzes, diagnose, and optionally corrects common hard-disk errors. Reports on the status of files on disk.

CHKDSK drive:\path\file(s) /switches

CLS Clears the screen.

CLS

COPY Copies and combines files.

COPY source:\path\file(s) target:\path\file(s) /switches

DATE Displays or sets the system date.

DATE date

DEL or ERASE Deletes files.

DEL drive:\path\file(s) /switches

ERASE drive:\path\file(s) /switches

DELTREE Removes a directory, including all its files and subdirectories.

DELTREE /switch drive:path

DIR Displays a list of files in a directory.

DIR drive:\path\file(s) /switches

DISKCOMP Compares the content of two floppy disks on a tarck-by-track basis, reporting which track numbers are not identical.

DISKCOMP source: target: /switches

DISKCOPY   Copies the content of one floppy disk to another on a track-by-track basis.

DISKCOPY source: target: /switches

DOSKEY   Allows DOS to remember DOS commands, and permits the user to move the cursor along the command line, editing DOS commands before they are invoked.

DOSKEY macro = commands [/options]

EDIT   Starts a full screen text editor.

EDIT drive:\path\file /D

FDISK   Partitions a hard disk for DOS.

FDISK /switch

FIND   Locates and displays all occurances of a specified character string in a specified file.

FIND /switches "string" drive:\path\file

FORMAT   Prepares a blank disk for receiving and storing data, or creates a new blank disk from a used one.

FORMAT target: /switches

LABEL   Adds or modifies a disk volume label.

LABEL target: label

MD or MKDIR   Creates a new subdirectory.

MD or MKDIR drive:\path directory

MODE   Performs various functions relating to the transfer of data between the processor, screen, printer and keyboard.

MODE cols=c lines=l

MORE   Forces DOS to display output one screen at a time instead of continous scrolling.

MORE < drive:\path\file(s)

Command [parameter(s)] | MORE

MOVE	Moves files to different locations. Can rename subdirectories. **MOVE source:\path\file(s) target:\path\file(s)**
MSBACKUP	Backs up and restores files. **MSBACKUP specific /switches**
PATH	Specifies a list of subdirectories where DOS is to look for executable program files. **PATH drive:\path; drive:\path ......**
PROMPT	Changes the appearance of the DOS system prompt. **PROMPT prompt string**
RD or RMDIR	Removes empty sub-directories. **RD or RMDIR drive:\path\subdirectory**
REN or RENAME	Changes file names **REN or RENAME drive:\path\oldfile drive:\path\newfile**
REPLACE	Selectively updates files on a target directory by replacing them with files od the same name on a source directory, or adds files to the target directory from the source. **REPLACE source:\path\file(s) target:\path /switches**
RESTORES	Restores files from disks made using the BACKUP command form earliar versions of DOS. **RESTORES source drive: target drive:[\path\file(s)] [/switches]**
SORT	Sorts data in character-based files or sorts the output of DOS commands. **SORT /switches < drive:\path\file**

	Command| SORT /switches
SYS	Copies DOS system files to a new disk. **SYS source:\path target:**
TIME	Displays and allows changes to the system time. **TIME hh:mm:ss.cc a/p**
TREE	Displays the subdirectory structure of a drive. **TREE drive:\path /switches**
TYPE	Displays the contents of a file. **TYPE drive:\path\file**
UNDELETE	Recovers accidently deleted files. **UNDELETE drive:\path\file(s) /switches**
VER	Displays the current DOS version number. **VER**
VERIFY	Enables/disables the verify switch for writing files during DOS operation. **VERIFY on/off**
VOL	Display the disk volume label. **VOL drive:**

APPENDIX B
CONFIGURING YOUR DOS

The CONFIG.SYS file is an ASCII text file that contains instructions to DOS regarding your system configuration. It resides in the root directory of the default starting drive and is read by DOS only once, at startup time.

Certain peripheral devices and applications require that you include commands in CONFIG.SYS. Other commands are used for such purpose as increasing disk-read buffers and maximum allowed number of open files, loading peripheral device software, and increasing the number of logical drive letters in your system.

BY PASSING CONFIG.SYS AND AUTOEXEC.BAT

On rare occasions you may need to start your computer without running the commands in CONFIG.SYS and AUTOEXEC.BAT You can use any of the three methods listed below to bypass startup commands.

- To by pass both CONFIG.SYS and AUTOEXEC.BAT Press F5 or press and hold down shift key as soon as you see the "Starting MS-DOS......" message when restarting your computer.

- To be asked whether you want to execute individual CONFIG.SYS commands and whether to run AUTOEXEC.BAT, Press F8 as soon as the "Starting MS-DOS......" message appears. You'll then be prompted to answer yes (Y) or No (N) before each command is executed.

- To have DOS confirm a specific CONFIG.SYS command each time your computer starts, follow the DEVICE command name with a question mark (?), as in device ? =C:\Windows\gmouse-sys.

BREAK

Controls when DOS checks for Ctrl-Break entered by the user.

Syntax

BREAK = ON/OFF

The Ctrl-Break or Ctrl-C key combinations cancel most DOS commands and some applications as well. Normally, DOS checks to see if the user entered Ctrl-Break or Ctrl-C only during functions that transmit data to and from the processor. BREAK=ON will cause DOS to check for cancellation during any DOS function call. This allows the operating system to cancel processing when commands or applications use very little data input and output.

BUFFERS

Sets the number of disk-read buffers.

Syntax

BUFFERS = ##,n

Where ## is the number of buffers to be used by DOS. The valid range is 1 to 99.

A buffer is an area of memory set aside for temporary data storage. Buffers can speed up system performance by reducing the number of times DOS must directly access the disk; however, each buffer takes up about 530 bytes of RAM, reducing the amount of memory available for processing. Too many buffers will slow a system down.

If you are trying to increase system performance by increasing the number of buffers, you might start with the following list, which relates buffers to the size of your hard disk :

Hard Disk Size (in MB)	Suggested Number of Buffers
20-32	20
40-80	30
80-120	40
120+	50

The n parameter specifies an additional number of read-ahead buffers, which store data just beyond the area of the disk being read, where n is the number of read-ahead buffers. DOS can anticipate upto 8 sectors of information on disk, so this number should be set to 8 in most cases. Read-ahead buffers further enhance system speed. Valid range is 0 to 8. Default is zero.

COUNTRY

Install international character sets and punctuation conventions.

Syntax

COUNTRY = Code, page, drive:\path\file.extension

Use the COUNTRY command to start your system with a non-United States keyboard and display character set.

The code parameter is a three-digit number. If this command is not used, the default country code is 001 (the united states). The country code specifies the time and date formats used by the commands MSBACKUP, DATA, RESTORE and TIME. Then optional page parameter is a three-digit number for each code page number in the COUNTRY.SYS file. If this parameter is not supplied, a default is used for each country code.

The COUNTRY.SYS file is the default file for country-specific data. This file must be located on the root directory if the file parameter is not used. Include the file parameter if you are using a file other than COUNTRY.SYS or if the country-specific data file is not located on the root directory.

Examples

COUNTRY=002 installs the French Canadian character set.
COUNTRY=002,C:\DOS\COUNTRY.SYS

installs the same character set, and specifies that the COUNTRY.SYS file can be found in the C:\DOS directory.

DEVICE

Installs device drivers.

Syntax

DEVICE = drive:\path\file/switches

Many peripheral devices and some applications require that a special controlling software program, called a device driver, be loaded in memory. By convention, many device drivers have the file extension .SYS. DOS includes a number of device drivers, each with their own special options for a discussion of these device drivers.

Use the DEVICE command, as instructed by your device driver documentation, to load the software program.

Example

DEVICE = ANSI.SYS

loads the extended keyboard and screen driver for example of other DOS device driver syntax.

(DETAILS OF DRIVER DETAIL HAS BEEN DISCUSSED IN APPENDIX C)*

DRIVPARM

Modifies disk drive parameters.

Syntax

DRIVPARM = /D:drive/switches

The DRIVPARM command requires that you specify a physical drive connected to your system, using the /D: switch, followed by a number indicating which drive is being reconfigured. Numbers are in the range 0-255, where O is drive A, 1 is drive B, 2 is drive C, and so forth. After specifying the drive to be reconfigured use other switches to indicates the new configuration for the drive.

Switches

/C   Indicates that the drive is capable of detecting whether the drive door has been opened and closed.

/F:type   Specifies the drive type, where type is a number indicating the drive type.

Valid values for type are :

0	= 180K or 360K (also 160K or 320K)
1	= 1.2Mb, 5.25"
2	= 720K, 3.5"
5	= Hard Disk
6	= Tape drive
7	= 1.44Mb, 3.5"
8	= Read/Write Optical Disk
9	= 2.88Mb, 3.5"

The default for the drive parameter is 2.

/H:heads   Specifies the number of read/write heads, where heads is a number in the range 1-99.

/I   Specifies a 3.5" floppy disk drive installed on your computer, if your system's ROM BIOS does not support 3.5" drives.

/N   Specifies a non-removable drive.

/S:sectors   Specifies the number of sectors per track, where sectors is a number in the range 1-99.

/T:tracks   Specifies the number of tracks per side, where tracks is the indicated number.

Example DRIVPARM=/D:4/F:6/H:1/s:80/t:16

specifies that Drive E is a tape drive, use 1 head, read 80 sectors per track, and 16 tracks.

DOS

Loads the operating system is conventional, extended, or reserved memory.

Syntax

DOS=high/low, umb, noumb

If you include this command in CONFIG.SYS, you must have previously loaded the HIMEM.SYS device driver using the DEVICE command. Refer to Appendix C for details regarding HIMEM.SYS. The UMB parameter is also required to use the DEVICEHIGH and LOADHIGH commands.

Use the HIGH parameter to load DOS into extended memory. By loading DOS in extended memory (that portion of RAM starting at 1024K), you can free a significant amount of system RAM for application software. You must have sufficient extended memory installed in your system to take advantage of this feature.

Example

DOS=HIGH, UMB

loads DOS into reserved memory, with any remainder placed in extended memory.

DOS=LOW, UMB

loads DOS into reserved memory, with any remainder placed in conventional memory.

This command is available only on 80386 or 80486 machines, and some advanced 80286 machines that are capable of mapping extended and reserved memory.

If you specify DOS=HIGH and DOS is unable to find or use the high memory area, it will display the following message.

HMA not available

Loading DOS low

FCBS

Specifies the number of open files using file control blocks.

Syntax

FCBS = maximum, open

The FCBS command is used primarily with networking schemes that control the number of open files by means of file control blocks, which are pointers to the location of open files on disk. Include this command in CONFIG.SYS if you are using a network, the SHARE command, or software that manages open files by this method, if your software documentation instructs you to do so.

The maximum parameter indicates the maximum number of open file control blocks, from 1 to 255. Default is 4.

The open parameter indicates the number of files that will not automatically close if processing attempts to open more files than allowed by the maximum parameter. If processing attempts to open more files than allowed by the FCBS command, DOS displays an error message.

Example

FCBS = 48, 8

specifies a maximum of 48 open file control blocks, with upto 8 files protected from automatic closing if processing attempts to open more than 48.

FCBS = 1,1

sets the maximum number of file control blocks to 1.

FILES

Sets the maximum allowed number of simultaneously open files.

Syntax

FILES=n

The n parameter indicates the maximum number of concurrently open files. Default is 8; maximum number is 255. If you exceed the maximum number of open files during processing, DOS displays the message "Too many files are open".

Example

FILES=25

indicates that a maximum of 25 files may be open at once.

INCLUDE

Invokes a series of CONFIG.SYS commands from another section of the file.

Syntax

INCLUDE=block

Use the INCLUDE command with a CONFIG.SYS file that contains multiple configurations. In a multiple-configuration CONFIG.SYS file, you can isolate and identify any series of commands that might be used in more than one configuration.

Example

Following is an example of a simple block of configuration commands that might appear in a CONFIG.SYS FILE. NOTICE THAT THE CONFIGURATION BLOCK NAME APPEARS WITHIN BRACKETS :

> **[EXPANDED-MEM]**
> **DEVICE=C:\DOS\HIMEM.SYS**
> **DEVICE=C:\DOS\EMM386.EXE RAM**
> **[exp-ramdisk]**
> **INCLUDE=expanded-mem**
> **DEVICEHIGH=C:\DOS\RAMDRIVE.SYS 1024/X**

Once this series of commands is so identified with configuration block names, a multiple configuration file that accesses the commands in the exp-ramdisk configuration block will access the commands in the expanded-mem block as well.

INSTALL

Loads terminate-and-stay-resident (TSR) software.

Syntax

INSTALL =[drive:\path\]file.extension

TSR programs are normally loaded by means of executable files at the DOS prompt. The INSTALL command lets you load TSR programs at the earliest point in the power-on process; this can help reduce conflicts by loading such programs in areas of memory where they are least likely to cause RAM addressing conflicts with other applications. Include a drive letter and sub-directory location if the executable files does not exist on the root directory. The file extension .COM or .EXE is required.

Four DOS external commands may be loaded this way : FASTOPEN.EXE, KEYB.COM, NLSFUNC.EXE, and SHARE.EXE.

Example

INSTALL = C:\DOS\SHARE.EXE

installs the SHARE command from the file located on the C:\DOS sub-directory.

LASTDRIVE

Specifies the largest logical drive letter to be used by the system.

Syntax

LASTDRIVE = drive

The drive parameter is a letter from A to Z. The colon is not used in this syntax.

This command alerts DOS that you will be using more logical drive letters than actual logical drives in the system.

Example

LASTDRIVE = H

sets a maximum of 8 logical drive letters.

MENUCOLOR

Specifies text and background colors for a configuration menu.

Syntax

MENUCOLOR=text,background

The MENUCOLOR command is used in a multiple-configuration CONFIG.SYS file to specify the text and background colors of the screen while a menu block is active. The text parameter is required. The background parameter is optional. The parameters are supplied as integers in the range 0-15 according to the following color codes :

Code	Color
0	Black
1	Blue
2	Green
3	Cyan
4	Red
5	Magenta
6	Brown
7	White
8	Gray
9	Bright Blue
10	Bright Green
11	Bright Cyan
12	Bright Red
13	Bright Magenta
14	Yellow
15	Bright White

Example

MENUCOLOR = 0,6

sets menu text as black, on a brown background.

MENUDEFAULT

Specifies a default configuration block and optional time-out value for accessing the default.

Syntax

MENUDEFAULT = block, time-out

Use this command within a menu block in a multiple-configuration CONFIG.SYS file. The block parameter is required, and must be the name of a block of configuration commands that are identified elsewhere in CONFIG.SYS. The time-out parameter is an integer in the range 0-90, indicating the number of seconds DOS will display the menu before automatically selecting the default.

Example

MENUDEFAULT = base, 15

Indicates that the default is a block of commands identified elsewhere as base and that DOS will wait 15 seconds before automatically selecting this configuration block.

MENUITEM

Identifies a block of CONFIG.SYS commands to be included in a configuration menu.

Syntax

MENUITEM = block, text

Use the MENUITEM command to identify available choices in a configuration menu in your CONFIG.SYS file. The block parameter is required, and specifies a block of configuration commands identified elsewhere in CONFIG.SYS. This block will be accessed if the user selects the indicated menu item. The text parameter is optional. It is a prompt that is displayed in the menu, detailing to the user the type of configuration that will be accessed if this menuitem is selected. The prompt may be up to seventy characters long.

Example

The following example is a menu block with three menu items :

[menu]

MENUITEM=WIN,WINDOW MODE

MENUITEM=rdisk2,RAM disk (2048) ORAC, ORACLE MODEL

MENUITEM=nordisk, No RAM disk, NORM, NORMAL MODE

Assume that your CONFIG.SYS file contains configuration blocks named rdiskl, rdisk2, and nordisk. This menu block will then cause DOS to display the following menu when you start your computer :

MS-DOS 6 Startup Menu

>   1. **RAM Disk (1024K)**
>
>   2. **RAM Disk (2048K)**
>
>   3. **No RAM Disk**
>
>   **Enter a choice :**

You may include upto nine menu items in a single configuration menu. If the specified block parameter does not exist in the CONFIG.SYS file, the menu item will not be included in the menu, and cannot be selected.

NUMLOCK

Turns the keyboard's numeric keypad on or off at startup time.

Syntax

NUMLOCK = ON/OFF

Use the NUMLOCK command within a menu block in a multiple configuration CONFIG.SYS file. The only valid parameter for the NUMLOCK command is either ON or OFF. If set to ON, DOS turns the numeric keypad on when the menu is displayed. If set to OFF, DOS turns the numeric keypad off.

Example

NUMLOCK = ON

ensures that the numeric keypad is on when the menu appears.

REM

Indicates a command line to be ignored by DOS.

SYNTAX

REM [command]

The REM command allows you to place comments in CONFIG.SYS for documenting the purposes of commands, or refreshing your memory if you return to edit the file after a long period of time. You can also use the REM command to "command out" certain CONFIG.SYS commands that you use only occasionally.

Example

REM the following loads the XMS extended memory controller

> **REM HIMEM.SYS (when the REM preceding DEVICE = is removed):**
>
> **REM DEVICE = C:\DOS\HIMEM.SYS**

The first two lines are a simple comment. On the third line, the REM command blocks loading of the HIMEM.SYS driver.

STACKS

Sets dynamic allocation of stack space.

Syntax

STACKS = frames.size

Dynamic stack spare allocation permits multiple interrupt calls to call each other without crashing the system.

The frames parameter sets the number of stack frames. Default is 9, except for IBM-PC, XT, or portable machines, where the default is 0. Valid numbers of frames are from 8 to 64. The size parameter indicates the size of each frame. Default is 128, except for IBM-PC, XT, or portable machines, where the default is 0. Valid frame sizes are from 32 to 512 bytes.

Example

STACKS = 18,128

increases the dynamic stack capacity to 18 frames, 128 bytes each.

STACKS = 0,0

turns off dynamic stack allocation.

SUBMENU

Specifies a submenu of additional choices within a menu block.

Syntax

SUBMENU = block, txt

The SUBMENU command is used within menu blocks in a multiple-configuration CONFIG.SYS file. The block parameter is required, and must be the name of a menu block defined elsewhere within the CONFIG.SYS file. This menu will be displayed if the user selects the indicated submenu. The text parameter is optional. It is a prompt that is displayed in the menu, detailing to the user what submenu will be accessed if this menu item is selected. The prompt may be upto seventy characters long.

Example

SUBMENU = alt-menu, Additional Configurations

will display an option to select a submenu block named alt-menu (provided it is defined in CONFIG.SYS), with the prompt, "Additional Configurations."

SWITCHES

Allows backward compatibility from 101-key keyboards, movement of the WINA20.386 file from the root directory, and control of DOS startup options.

Syntax

SWITCHES = /switches

Switches

/K   Causes the keyboard to emulate an older style keyboard on the system.

/N   Disables function keys F5 and F8.

/F   Disables the timed delay after displaying the message "Starting MS-DOS...." Use this switch to save a little time if you have also used the /N switch.

APPENDIX C
DEVICE DRIVER FILES

DOS 6.0 includes twelve standard device driver files for use in creating optional system configurations. These device drivers control memory allocations, display options, and disk drive usage. These are

ANSI.SYS	DISPLAY.SYS	DRIVER.SYS
DBLSPACE.SYS	EGA.SYS	EMM386.SYS
HIMEM.SYS	INTERLNK.EXE	POWER.EXE
RAMDRIVE.SYS	SETVER.EXE	SMARTDRV.EXE

These drivers are all loaded into memory using the DEVICE command in the CONFIG.SYS file, These can also be loaded using DEVICEHIGH command, provided that you have previously loaded HIMEM.SYSand EMM386.SYS.

ANSI.SYS

Extended screen and keyboard device driver.

Syntax

DEVICE = drive:\path\ANSI.SYS/switches

This driver loads extended capabilities for adapting the screen display and modifying the keyboard keys, to be used by applications that require these features.

	Fn	Shift-Fn	Ctrl-Fn	Alt-Fn
F1	0;59	0;84	0;94	0;104
F2	0;60	0;85	0;95	0;105
F3	0;61	0;86	0;96	0;106
F4	0;62	0;87	0;97	0;107
F5	0;63	0;88	0;98	0;108
F6	0;64	0;89	0;99	0;109
F7	0;65	0;90	0;100	0;110

F8	0;66	0;91	0;101	0;111
F9	0;67	0;92	0;102	0;112
F10	0;68	0;93	0;103	0;113
F11	0;133	0;135	0;137	0;139
F12	0;134	0;136	0;138	0;140

Switches

/X   Enables keyboard redefinition features for duplicate keys on the newer, 101-key   keyboard. This switch does not load ANSI.SYS into extended memory.

/K   Ignores extended keys on 101-keys keyboards. If you have used the SWITCHES   /K command in CONFIG.SYS, use this switch with ANSI.SYS.

Example

DEVICE = C:\DOS\ANSI.SYS/X

loads the full set of ANSI keyboard and screen redefinition functions.

The following Examples show ANSI escape sequences that can be entered by means of batch files once you have loaded the ANSI.SYS driver.

ECHO ESC[0;67;"COPY"*.* A:"P

ECHO ESC[0;67;"COPY*.* B:"P

redefines the F9 function key to invoke the command COPY *.* A: and the F10 function key to invoke the command COPY *.* B:.

DEFAULT VALUES OF FUNCTION KEYS

F1   Displays template one character at a time

F2   Displays template up to next character typed

F3   Displays all remaining characters in template

F4   Displays character after next character typed

F5   Makes command line new template

F6   Ctrl-Z

F1   will display the last command line, or template, one character at a time. The right arrow key has the same function.

F2   followed by a character, will display template up to, but not including the, character.

F3   will display all the remaining characters in the template.

F4   followed by a character, the template is displayed starting with the character immediatly after the first occurance of the character.

DISPLAY.SYS

Loads international font sets for the screen display.

Syntax

DEVICE =drive:\path\DISPLAY.SYS

CON = [type, codepage, additional, subfont]

ANSI Key Codes - Extended Keyboard Keys

Keypad Keys	K	Shift-K	Ctrl-K	Alt-L
/	47	47	0;142	0;74
*	42	42	0;144	0;78
-	45	45	0;149	0;164
+	43	43	0;150	0;55
5	53	53	0;76	0;143

Extended (Gray) Keys

	K	Shift-K	Ctrl-K	Alt-K
á	224;72	224;72	224;141	224;152
â	224;80	224;80	224;145	224;154
ß	224;75	224;75	224;115	224;155
à	224;77	224;77	224;116	224;157
Delete	224;83	224;83	224;147	224;163

End	224;79	224;79	224;117	224;159
Home	224;71	224;71	224;119	224;151
Insert	224;82	224;82	224;146	224;162
Page Down	224;81	224;81	224;118	224;161
Page Up	224;73	224;73	224;132	224;153

To specify an international character set using the DISPLAY.SYS driver, indicate a display type as well as at least one character set code page. The type parameter is one of the following :

EGA   Enhanced graphics adapter, also VGA displays

LCD   PC Convertible adapter

The codepage parameter is a three-digit number representing international character sets. Valid numbers are :

437   United States

850   Multilingual (Latin I)

852   Slavic (Latin II)

860   Portuguese

863   Canadian-French

865   Nordic

E.g.

DEVICE = C:\DOS\DISPLAY.SYS CON=(EGA,863,1)

loads the Canadian screen display font set and specifies that one additional font set will be prepared using the MODE command.

DRIVER.SYS

Assigns logical drive letters to floppy disk drives.

Syntax

DEVICE = drive:\path\DRIVER.SYS/switches

Each time this command is invoked, DOS assigns the next available floppy disk drive letter to the specified device. The switches allow you to specify exact formatting requirements for the new logical drive. You can assign additional drive letters to the same or other devices by repeating this command in CONFIG.SYS.

Switches

/D:n   Indicates the drive number, where n is a number from 0 to 127.0 refers to the A drive, 1 to B drive, and so forth. Additional floppy disk drives must be external. On a system with one internal floppy disk drive, O refers to both drive A and B. This switch is required and should be supplied first.

/C   Enables change-line support, a feature that allows DOS to detect if a floppy disk has been changed in the drive during operations. Default is no change line support.

/F:n   Specifies the drive format, where n is a number indicating one of the following formats :

         0 =   160K/180K or 320K/360K 5.25"n

         1 =   1.2 megabyte 5.25"

         2 =   720 K 3.5"

         7 =   1.44 Mb 3.5"

         9 =   2.88 Mb 3.5"

         The default value is 2.

/H:nn   Indicates the number of heads per drive, where nn is a number from 1 to 99.

/S:nn   Indicates the number of sectors per track, where nn is a number from 1 to 99. Defaults depend on the specified drive type, as follows:

     /S:9 =   360K and lower, 720K 3.5"

     /Sl:15=   1.2Mb 5.25"

/S:18=   1.44Mb 3.5"

/S:36=   2.88Mb 3.5"

/T:nn   Indicates the number of tracks on each side, where nn is a number from 1 to 99. Default is 80, except for disks that are 360 K and lower, in which case the default is 40.

E.g.

DEVICE = C:\DOS\DRIVER.SYS/D:1/T:80/S:9/H:2/F:2

assigns the next available drive letter to drive B, and indicates that it is to be treated as a 3.5", 720 K drive. Assuming that you have a system with two floppy drives and a single hard disk, this command would allow drive B to function as both drive B and drive D. Thus, you could copy disks in the same drive by entering the command COPY B:*.* D:, and DOS would prompt you to switch disks as required to make the copy.

DBLSPACE.SYS

Specifies the memory location of the compressed-data operating system driver named DBLSPACE.BIN.

Syntax

DEVICEHIGH = drive:\path\DBLSPACE.SYS /switch

DOS automatically loads DBLSPACE.BIN, along with the operating system, at start-up. Since it is loaded before other drivers that manage upper memory, it is initially loaded in conventional memory. Use the DEVICEHIGH command in CONFIG.SYS, along with the /MOVE switch, to move the compressed-data driver to upper memory.

Switches

/MOVE   Moves DBLSPACE.BIN from the top of conventional memory (its default location) to the bottom when used with the DEVICE command.

E.g.

DEVICEHIGH =C:\DOS\DBLSPACE.SYS /MOVE

moves DBLSPACE.BIN to upper memory. EMM386.EXE must be previously loaded for this command to work.

EGA.SYS

Driver which saves and restore EGA screens used with the DOS Shell Task Swapper.

Syntax

DEVICE = drive:\path\EGA.SYS

This driver loads saving and restoring capabilities for EGA screens. Use this driver if your system has trouble handling screen displays when moving between programs in the DOS Shell. There are no switches and its functions are transparent to the user.

E.g.

DEVICE = C:\DOS\EGA.SYS

loads the EGA screen saver functions when the EGA.SYS file is stored on the C:\DOS sub-directory.

EMM386.EXE

Installs expanded and reserved memory support for 80386 and 80486 computer systems with extended memory.

Syntax

DEVICE = drive :\path\EMM386.EXE size ON/OFF/AUTO RAM/NOEMS/switches

The EMM386.EXE expanded-memory manager should be installed only after HIMEM.SYS (extended-memory manager) is installed. Do not load this driver using the DEVICEHIGH command. The DEVICEHIGH command is valid only after this driver is completely loaded.

Switches

Size

Required only if you intend to configure a portion of your system's total extended memory as expanded memory, where size is a number indicating the expanded memory size in kilobytes (e.g., 64 equals 64K).

If you leave out this parameter and the NOEMS parameter, upto 32768K (or the amount available on your system, whichever is less) of extended memory will be used as expanded memory. If you specify NOEMS, default size is 0.

AUTO

Loads the Expanded Memory driver, but activates the driver only when a program calls for expanded memory.

E.g.

DEVICE = X:\DOS\EMM386.EXE 1024 RAM

enables expanded-memory support for 1Mb of expanded memory, plus reserved-memory support.

DEVICE=C:\DOS\EMM386.EXE RAM NOEMS

enables support for reserved memory only.

MESSAGES in loading CONFIG.SYS

EMM386 installed

Extended memory allocated	**: XXXXXkB**
System memory allocated	**: XXXXXkB**
Expanded memory available	**: XXXXXkB**
Page frame base address	**: XX000kB**

This message appears just after EMM386.SYS is loaded into memory. The message displays the amount of expanded memory available and the address where EMM386.SYS has located its page frame. The amount of expanded memory available is the sum of the extended memory and system memory EMM386.SYS has reclaimed.

Invalid parameter specified

During installation, a parameter other than those documented above or an incorrect parameter has been specified.

Size of expanded memory pool adjusted

Less extended memory is available than was requested through the size parameter during installation.

Option ROM or RAM detected within page frame

This warning occurs when forcing the EMM386.SYS page frame into the desired memory location by using Mx option. You were trying to force the page frame into an area already used by an expansion option board.

EMM386 not installed - insufficient memory

You will need additional extended memory required to install EMM386.SYS.

EMM386 not installed - incorrect DOS version

You have tried to install EMM386.SYS on a machine using a version of MS-DOS lower than 3.1.

EMM386 not installed - incorrect machine type

EMM386.SYS can only run on 80386 machine or compatible.

EMM386 already installed

You can't install EMM386.SYS twice.

HIMEM.SYS

Loads extended memory support using Microsoft's XMS extended memory specification.

Syntax

DEVICE=drive:\path\HIMEM.SYS/switches

Use HIMEM.SYS to enable extended memory support for all DOS commands that make use of RAM above 1024K. Such CONFIG.SYS commands include EMM386.EXE, DOS=HIGH, as well as any device drive that is loaded into extended memory.

/HMAMIN=nn   Specifies the amount of memory an application must use before having access to extended memory, where nn is the amount of memory in kilobytes. The valid range is 0-63K. Default is O, meaning that HIMEM.SYS will allocate extended memory to the first application that requires it.

/NT15=nnnn   Specifies the amount of extended memory HIMEM.SYS will ignore for XMS support, where nnnn is a number representing the amount of memory in kilobytes. This switch allows HIMEM.SYS to reserve a portion of extended memory for use by programs that require extended memory but are not compatible with the XMS memory specification HIMEM.SYS uses.

Default is zero.

/NUM-HANDLE=nnn

Specifies how many memory block handles can be used simultaneously, where nnn is the number of handles. The valid range is 1-128 handles. Default is 32. This switch has no effect when running Windows in enhanced mode.

/SHADOWRAM ON/OFF

Disables shadow RAM on some computers that support this feature and adds the memory used by shadow RAM back to available memory when set to OFF. When set to ON, HIMEM.SYS ignores shadow RAM. Default is OFF if your computer has less than 1Mb of extended memory.

/V Displays status and error messages during loading.

E.g.
DEVICE=C:\DOS\HIMEM.SYS

enables XMS extended memory support for all available extended memory.

DEVICE=C:\DOS\HIMEM.SYS/INT15=2048

enables XMS extended memory support for all memory, reserving 2048K for other programs not compatible with XMS.

MESSAGES in loading HIMEM.SYS

64 High Memory Area is available

You have installed HIMEM.SYS properly.

ERROR : HIMEM.SYS requires DOS 3.00 or higher.
XMS driver not installed.

You have tried to installed HIMEM.SYS on a machine using a version of MS-DOS lower than 3.00.

ERROR : HIMEM.SYS requires an 80X86 -based machine.
XMS driver not installed.

You have tried to install HIMEM.SYS on a machine other than 80286 or higher machine.

ERROR : An Extended memory Manager is already installed

XMS driver not installed.

You have tried to install HIMEM.SYS after it has been already installed on computer.

ERROR : No available extended memory was found.

You are trying to install HIMEM.SYS on a computer without Extended Memory.

ERROR : Unrecognized A20 hardware

HIMEM.SYS can't recognize the A20 hardware of your system. If this occurs, it is probably because the system is not the one supported by this release of HIMEM.SYS.

WARNING : The high memory area is unavailable

Himem.SYS can't find enough memory to see the High Memory Area. HIMEM.SYS will not be able to process any request for the High Memory Area. However, HIMEM.SYS will remian installed to process any request for the extended Memory Data Blocks.

INTERLNK.EXE

Directs instructions to drives or printer ports on the Interlink server.

Syntax

DEVICE = drive:\path\INTERLNK.EXE/switches

Install the INTERLNK.EXE device driver on networked systems in order to use the INTERLNK and INTERSVR line commands.

Switches

/DRIVES:n	Specifies the number of redirected drives, where n is the number. Specify 0 to redirect printers only. Default is 3.
/NOPRINTER	Disables printer redirection.

/COMn/address   Specifies a serial port for data transfer, where n is the number of the port (104). Alternatively, use the address parameter to specify the address of the serial port if it is non-standard. If you omit both parameters, DOS uses the first port it finds connected to the server. If you omit this switch as well as the /LPT switch, DOS scans all ports.

/LPTn/address   Specifies a parallel port for data transfer, where n is the number of the port (1-3). Alternatively, use the address parameter to specify the address of the parallel port if it is non-standard. If you omit both parameters, DOS uses the first port it finds connected to the server.

/AUTO   Attempts to establish a connection with the server when the client starts up.

/NOSCAN   Disables attempts to establish a connection with the server when INTERLNK.EXE is installed. Default is to attempt to establish the connection.

/BAUD:rate   Forces maximum baud rate for serial data transfer. Valid rates are : 9600, 19200, 38400, 57600 and 115200. Default is 115200.

/V   Ignores timer conflicts.

E.g.

DEVICE=C:\DPS\INTERLNK.EXE/COM1/NOPRINTER

loads the Interlink driver to use COM1 and specifies that printer ports are not being redirected.

POWER.EXE

Lowers the rate of power consumption when devices are idle.

Syntax

DEVICE=drive:\path\POWER.EXE ADV:level STD/OFF/ switch

Use the DEVICE command to load this driver. The DEVICEHIGH command has no effect. By default, POWER.EXE attempts to load into upper memory.

Use the ADV:parameter to indicate your desired level of power conservation, where level is one of the following :

MAX   Conserves greatest amounts of power; Performance may be affected.

REG   Balances power conservation with performance. This is the default.

MIN   Conserves least amount of power, allowing near-full performance.

The STD parameter forces POWER.EXE to use the hardware's power-management features, if these features support the Advanced Power Management (APM) specification. If your hardware does not support APM, this parameter turns POWER.EXE off.

Alternatively, you can use the OFF parameter to turn off power management at startup time.

Switch

/LOW   Forces DOS to load POWER.EXE device driver in conventional memory.

RAMDRIVE.SYS

Initializes a RAM disk.

Syntax

DEVICE = drive"\path\RAMDRIVE.SYS size sectors directory/switch

A RAM disk simulates a disk drive in RAM, RAM disks tend to be faster than physical drives, although the fastest hard disks can run almost as fast.. RAM disks are also valuable when programs access the disk drive frequently, reducing drive wear as well as saving time.

RAM disks are volatile, however, you must save the data on a RAM disk to a physical drive before turning off the power failure while running a RAM disk, all data that was not saved to a physical disk will be lost.

The size parameter indicates the storage area of the RAM disk, expressed in kilobytes. Default is 64, for 64K . The sectors parameter indicates the size of a disk sector, expressed in bytes. Default is 512 bytes. The directory parameter indicates the maximum number of directory entries, from 2 to 1024. Default is 64.

/A   Stores the RAM disk in expanded memory.

/E   Stores the RAM disk in extended memory.

E.g.

DEVICE = C:\DOS\RAMDRIVE.SYS 2048 512 1024/E

installs a RAM disk in extended memory. Disk size is 2 Mb (2048K); sector size is 512 bytes; maximum number of directory entries is 1024.

SETVER.EXE

Installs a list of software applications that require DOS to supply an earlier version number.

Syntax

DEVICE = drive:\path\SETVER.EXE

The command to load the SETVER.EXE driver is automatically added to your CONFIG.SYS file when you install DOS 6. This command causes DOS to load a list of applications that require earlier version numbers.

SMARTDRV.EXE

Installs double-buffering for a SMARTDrive cache.

Syntax

DEVICE = drive:\path\SMARTDRV.DEX/DOUBLE_BUFFER

A disk cache improves system performance by storing the locations of frequently accessed files in memory, thereby reducing the overall number of disk accesses.

However SMARTDrive can also perform double-buffering, which allows some hard disk controllers to work with SMARTDrive under expanded memory (as configured by EMM386.EXE) or when running Windows in enhanced mode.

Switch

/DOUBLE_BUFFER   Instructs DOS to use SMARTDrive's double-buffering feature.

E.g.

DEVICE=C:\DOS\SMARTDRV.EXE/DOUBLE_BUFFER

loads the double-buffering feature, assuming SMARTDRV.EXE is on the C:\DOS directory.

APPENDIX D
DOS ERROR MESSAGES

ABORT, RETRY, IGNORE, FAIL ?

DOS failed to recognize an instruction it was given, or a disk or device error has prevented the instruction from being carried out. This message appears along with many of the other error messages in this appendix. You may choose one of four responses, as follows :

Abort   Press A to terminate the program entirely and return to the DOS prompt.

Retry   Press R to repeat the instruction. This works in cases where you can make a change in the system (for example, closing a disk-drive door), or when a momentary pause will allow a conflict to resolve itself (for example, waiting for the printer to warm up and come on-line). If you press R a few times and continue to receive this message, Press A.

Ignore   Press I to continue with processing, as if the error had not occurred. This option is risky, and is not recommended unless you are a software developer testing a program or are absolutely certain that continued processing will not have destructive results.

Fail   Press F to cancel the problematic instruction but continue with processing. Like Ignore, this is a risky option, because ignoring this instruction can cause unexpected results later on. Use it only if you know for certain what will happen.

ACCESS DENIED :

You attempted to open a file that is either labeled read-only, stored on a write-protected disk, or locked on a network. This message also appears if you use the TYPE command on a sub-directory or the CD or CHDIR command on a file. Use the ATTRIB command to remove the file's read-only status, remove the write protection from the disk, or change the file name specification, and then try again.

ALL FILES IN DIRECTORY
WILL BE DELETED ! ARE YOU SURE ?

You are about to delete all the files in the specified directory or the currently logged directory. Enter Y if you intend to do this; other wise, Enter N.

ATTEMPT TO REMOVE CURRENT DIRECTORY

You invoked the RD or RMDIR commands using the name of the currently logged directory. Log onto the parent directory and try again. You cannot remove the root directory.

BAD COMMAND OR FILE NAME

DOS did not recognize the command you entered at the DOS prompt. Check to make sure that you have entered the command correctly and that the command file can be found either on the specified directory or on the search path indicated by the PATH command.

BAD OR MISSING COMMAND INTERPRETER

You have attempted to load a version of COMMAND.COM that is not compatible with the current operating system, or COMMAND.COM cannot be found. Reboot, using a bootable floppy disk if necessary. Check that the correct version of COMMAND.COM is on the root directory, and that the correct version of COMMAND.COM has been specified using the SHELL command in CONFIG.SYS. Refer to the Format command in Part Four for details on creating a bootable floppy disk.

BAD OR MISSING DRIVER

DOS cannot locate the device driver file, or the file has become corrupted. Copy the driver file from backup onto the root directory or specify the location of the file on the initialization line in CONFIG.SYS.

BAD OR MISSING KEYBOARD DEFINITION FILE

DOS could not find the KEYBOARD.SYS file, or it has become corrupted. Be sure that KEYBOARD.SYS is located on the same directory as KEYB.EXE. If necessary, copy a new KEYBOARD.SYS file from backup.

BATCH FILE MISSING

Usually this message appears after a batch file has erased itself. Rewrite the batch file or restore it using the UNDELETE Command. Edit the batch file, using extra care with batch file commands that delete files, especially if they include wild card parameters.

CANNOT CHDIR TO PATH

CHKDSK cannot verify the existence of a sub-directory reported in the FAT. Run CHKDSK with the /F option to correct the problem.

CANNOT CHDIR TO ROOT

CHKDSK cannot locate the start of the root directory. Reboot the computer and re-invoke the command. If the problem continues, back up what files you can, if any, and reformat the disk.

CANNOT FIND SYSTEM FILES

You have attempted to load the operating system from a drive that does not contain system files. Use the SYS command to copy the system files to the drive and restore backup copies of CONFIG.SYS and AUTOEXEC.BAT to the root directory if necessary. If you cannot restore the system files, boot from a floppy disk, backup your data and reformat the disk using the FORMAT /S command.

CANNOT LOAD COMMAND, SYSTEM HALTED

An application has overwritten all or part of COMMAND.COM in memory, and DOS is unable to reload the command processor. Another possibility it that the COMSPEC environment variable has been reset to a nonexistent path name for COMMAND.COM. Reboot the computer, using the F8 function key if necessary. Check the integrity of the data modified by the application. If necessary copy COMMAND.COM to another directory and set the COMSPEC variable to that directory in AUTOEXEC.BAT.

CANNOT SETUP EXPANDED MEMORY

See the "Cannot load COMMAND" error message entry.

CONVERT LOST CHAINS TO FILES?

CHKDSK has discovered lost chains, which are areas of the disk that include data not assigned to files in the FAT. Answer Y to this question if you would like to recover this disk space. CHKDSK will convert the lost chains to files, giving them the name FILEnnnn. CHK, where nnnn is a number from 0000 to 9999. You can review, edit, rename, or delete these files as you wish.

CURRENT DRIVE IS NO LONGER VALID

The currently lodged drive does not have a disk in it, the drive door is open, or the drive is unrecognizable on a network. Change to another drive with a disk in it. Insert a disk in the drive. Close the drive door.

DATA ERROR

DOS has detected inconsistencies in data while reading or writing a file. You are prompted to Abort or Retry the operation. Press R (Retry) a few times, but if the message persists, press A (Abort). Check the disk using the CHKDSK command. Make fresh backups of the data (do not overwrite current backups) and reformat the disk. If the problem persists or occurs on several disks, have the drive serviced.

DIRECTORY ALREADY EXISTS

You have attempted to create a directory using the MD or MKDIR commands, but a directory of the same name is already on your system. Use a different name or another nesting level.

DRIVE OR DISKETTE TYPES NOT COMPATIBLE

You have attempted to use the DISKCOMP or DISKCOPY commands on drives with two different format types. Use the FC on XCOPY commands instead.

DUPLICATE FILE NAME

You have attempted to rename a file to the name of an existing file or directory. Use a different name.

DUPLICATE REDIRECTION

You have used the redirection symbols to read data from a file being written to. Revise the syntax using a unique output file name.

ERROR IN EXE FILE

The application's executable file contains errors that interfere with processing. The file may be incompatible with your current version of DOS. Check for the correct DOS version; if the version is correct, copy a new executable file from backup copies or the master disk. If the problem persists, discard the executable files.

ERROR LOADING OPERATING SYSTEM

The operating system files cannot be found or have become corrupted. Use the SYS command to copy the system files to the drive and copy the CONFIG.SYS and AUTOEXEC.BAT files to the root directory if necessary. If you cannot restore the system files, boot from a floppy disk, back up your data, and reformat the disk using the FORMAT/S command.

ERROR READING DIRECTORY

The file allocation table or sub-directory structure has become corrupted. Backup whatever data you can on blank diskettes; do not overwrite previous backups. Reformat the disk. If the problem persists, have the drive serviced.

ERROR READING SYSTEM FILE

One of the operating system files has become corrupted. Backup your data, if possible. Restart your system. If you cannot restart, reinstall the operating system. If the problem persists, have your hardware serviced.

ERROR READING (OR WRITING) TO DEVICE

The peripheral device could not accept data being sent to it, or DOS was unable to process data sent from the device. Check that the device is on line, that the baud rate at which you are sending data is not too fast, and that the data being sent is appropriate for the device; for example, do not send data at 0\9600 baud if the device can only process 1200 baud, and do not send binary files to a device that can accept only ASCII files.

ERROR READING (OR READING) DRIVE

This message usually indicates a corrupted disk in the drive. Try another disk; if the problem persists, try rebooting the system. If the problem continues, have the drive serviced.

EXPANDED MEMORY MANAGER NOT PRESENT

You must install the expanded memory manager before installing drivers that require this memory. Move the expanded memory manager initialization line to an earlier position in the CONFIG.SYS file.

FAIL ON INT 24

DOS has encountered a unrecoverable critical error during processing for example, a mechanical drive failure or corrupted file. If the computer has stopped altogether, try to restart. If you can replicate the problem, delete the files that cause the problem or have the part serviced.

FILE ALLOCATION TABLE BAD

The file allocation table has become corrupted. Backup whatever data that you can on blank diskettes. Do not overwrite previous backups. You may solve the problem by invoking the CHKDSK command. If necessary reformat the disk. If the problem persists, have the drive serviced.

FILE CANNOT BE COPIED ONTO ITSELF

You have specified the same file as both the source and target. This often happens when wild card characters have not been used carefully. Change the file specification for the source or target as necessary, and try again.

FILE CREATION ERROR

One of the following has happened :

- There was not enough space on the disk or chosen sub-directory for the file you tried to create.
- The file you tried to create already exists and is read-only.
- You tried to rename a file using a file name that already exists.

-   You attempted to redirect output to an invalid filename. Refer to Part One for details on valid names for files.

If the file is on the root directory, check that the maximum number of root directory files (512) has not been reached. If the root directory (or entire disk) is full, delete some other files and try again. If the file in question is read-only, use a different target name, a different directory location, or use the ATTRIB command to remove the read-only attribute. You may be attempting to overwrite a hidden file; try a different target name or location. Also, if you are renaming files, use a different target name or location.

FILE IS CROSS-LINKED

CHKDSK has found two files that share the same area of the disk. If you have specified the /F option, the named file is truncated to remove the discrepancy.

FILE NOT FOUND

The requested file was not found on the currently logged directory or any of the directories specified with the PATH or APPEND COMMANDS. This message will also appear if the specified sub-directory is empty. Check the file name for correct spelling and correct location. If necessary, change the search path.

GENERAL FAILURE

The disk in the drive was not formatted or was formatted for a system other than DOS. Reformat the disk. If the problem continues, have the drive serviced.

INCORRECT DOS VERSION

You entered a DOS external command for a version that is different from the DOS version currently in RAM. Reboot with the correct version of DOS, or use the correct executable file for the command.

INCORRECT NUMBER OF PARAMETERS

See the "Invalid parameter" error message entry.

INSUFFICIENT DISK SPACE

You have used up all the available space on your disk for copying or creating files. Run CHKDSK to reclaim space that may be occupied by lost cluster. If necessary, delete some files.

INSUFFICIENT MEMORY

You do not have sufficient RAM to process the command you entered. Remove some memory resident files. Reboot the computer if necessary. Add more RAM to your system to accommodate the application or command.

INTERMEDIATE FILE ERROR DURING PIPE

A temporary file, created during a piping operation, has become corrupted. The disk may be too full, too many files may be open or a hardware problem has prevented successful processing. Run CHKDSK to determine if problems exist on the data drive. Delete unnecessary files to make room on the disk. Make sure the disk is not write-protected. If too many files were open, change the FILES command in CONFIG.SYS and reboot the computer.

INTERNAL ERROR

A memory conflict or other technical error has occurred. Reboot the computer. If you detect a pattern to the appearance of the error, restore the problem application or DOS file from backup or reinstall the file from master disks and try it again. If the message appears randomly, have the computer serviced by a qualified technician. Do not overwrite current backups with new backups after seeing this message until the cause is determined and the problem solved.

INVALID COMMAND.COM

See the "Bad or missing command interpreter" error message entry.

INVALID DATE

DOS cannot recognize the date format you have entered, or you have entered a nonexistent date. Check your entry and try again.

INVALID DIRECTORY

You have entered an invalid directory name or the name of a directory that does not exist, or DOS has discovered an invalid directory on the disk. Check the spelling of the directory name and reenter it if it is incorrect. If the invalid directory was discovered by DOS, backup what files you can onto fresh backup disks. Do not overwrite current backups. Reformat or replace the disk.

INVALID DRIVE SPECIFICATION

You have entered the letter of a drive that does not exist. Enter a different drive letter or assign the drive letter using the ASSIGN or SUBST command.

INVALID PARAMETER

You have not specified the correct option switches on the command line, or have duplicated parameters, or have combined parameters illegally. Review the correct syntax of the command and try it again.

INVALID PARTITION TABLE

DOS has detected an error in the fixed disk's partition information. Backup whatever data you can and run FDISK to initialize a valid partition table.

INVALID PATH

You invoked the RD or RMDIR commands using the name of the currently logged directory. Log onto the parent directory and try again. You cannot remove the root directory.

You have specified a nonexistent directory, or one that DOS cannot find. Check the drive and path specification, the spelling of the directory name, and the settings of the PATH and APPEND commands.

INVALID PATH, NOT
DIRECTORY, OR DIRECTORY NOT EMPTY

DOS is not able to locate the specified directory, or you entered a file in place of a directory name, or the directory contains files (or other nested sub-directories) and cannot be removed. Check the spelling of the directory name or list the contents of the directory. If it appears empty, it may contain hidden files. Use the DIR/A:H command to reveal any possibly hidden files.

INVALID SWITCH

See the "Invalid parameter" error message entry.

INVALID SYNTAX

DOS could not process the syntax you entered. Review the correct command syntax and try again.

INVALID TIME

DOS cannot recognize the time format you have entered. Check your entry and try again.

NO EXTENDED MEMORY AVAILABLE

The XMS extended memory has been allocated to other applications and resident functions. Deactivate other drives to make room for your RAM disk.

NO FIXED DISKS PRESENT

DOS was not able to detect the presence of a fixed disk drive. Check your computer's setup parameters for the correct drive type. If necessary, perform a low-level format and repartition the disk drive. If you cannot solve the problem yourself, have the computer serviced by a competent technician.

NON-SYSTEM DISKS OR DISK ERROR

DOS cannot find system files on the current disk. Insert a disk containing system files or boot from the hard disk if it contains system files.

PATH NOT FOUND

See the "Invalid path" error message entry.

PRINTER ERROR

DOS cannot send data to your printing device. Make sure the device is on-line, has paper ready, and that the output has not been redirected to a different port.

READ FAULT ERROR

DOS cannot read data on the disk. Reinsert the disk in the drive and press R (Retry). If the error persists, run CHKDSK on the disk; if the disk is unrecoverable, reformat or discard it.

REQUIRED FONT NOT LOADED

DISPLAY.SYS has not been initialized to include the desired font. Edit CONFIG.SYS, increasing the number of subfonts, and reboot the computer.

SECTOR NOT FOUND

DOS has discovered a formatting error on the disk. If DOS allows it, back up the file being accessed at the time this message appeared to recover whatever portion may still be usable. Run CHKDSK to try to solve the disk's problems. If the problem persists, reformat or discard the disk.

SEEK ERROR

See the "Read fault error" error message entry.

TOO MANY FILES OPEN

See the "Too many open files" error message entry.

TOO MANY OPEN FILES

You have exceeded the maximum number of allowed open files on your system. Increase the maximum with the FILES command in CONFIG.SYS and reboot the computer.

TOO MANY REDIRECTIONS

You have redirected data output to a device that does not exist or have attempted to redirect data that has already been redirected. Correct the command line syntax for the correct device or a single redirection and try again.

TRACK 0 BAD

DOS has detected disk errors in a critical portion of the disk. Reboot the computer and try accessing the disk again. If the problem persists, discard the disk. If the problem occurs for an inordinate number of disks, have your floppy drive serviced.

UNABLE TO CREATE DIRECTORY

You have attempted to create a directory using the MD or MKDIR commands, but either a directory of the same name is already on your system, you have reached the limit on the number of entries in your root directory, or your disk is write-protected. Use a different name or try to create the directory at another nesting level.

UNRECOGNIZED COMMAND IN CONFIG.SYS

DOS could not recognize a command in the CONFIG.SYS file when booting. Other messages that appear before this one may help you determine which lines are invalid. Edit CONFIG.SYS and correct the invalid lines. If you are editing CONFIG.SYS with a word processor, be sure that you have the file as an ASCII file.

UNRECOVERABLE READ OR WRITE ERROR

DOS could not read or write data to the disk. The disk is probably damaged. Use a different disk to save the current data. Run CHKDSK on the damaged disk to attempt to recover what files you can. Reformat or discard the bad disk.

WARNING ! INVALID PARAMETER IGNORED

DOS cannot recognize a parameter you have entered on the HIMEM initialization line in CONFIG.SYS. Edit this line in the CONFIG.SYS file and reboot the computer.

WARNING ! NO FILES WERE FOUND TO RESTORE

Your file specification did not match files on the backup floppy disk. Log onto the target sub-directory before invoking the command. Review the command syntax carefully, and reenter the command with the correct file path specification for the hard disk. Refer to the RESTORE command in Part Four for detailed syntax information.

WRITE FAULT ERROR

DOS cannot write data to the disk. Reinsert the disk in the drive, and press R (Retry). If the error persists, run CHKDSK on the disk, if the disk is unrecoverable, discard it.

WRITE PROTECT ERROR

DOS cannot write data to the disk because it is write-protected. Remove the write-protection tab from the disk, reinsert the disk in the drive, and press R (Retry). If the error persists, use a different disk.

APPENDIX E
GLOSSARY

8086	An Intel Microprocessor with 16-bit data bus, and a 20-bit address bus. It can operate only in real mode.
8088	An Intel Microprocessor with 16-bit registers, an 8-bit data bus, and a 20-bit address but. It can operate only in real mode. This processor was designed as a low-cost version of the 8086.
80286	An Intel Microprocessor with 16-bit register, a 16-bit data bus, and a 24-bit address bus. It can operate in real and protected modes.
80386	An Intel Microprocessor with 32-bit registers, a 32-bit data bus, and a 32-bit address bus. It can operate in real-protected and virtual real modes.
80386SX	An Intel Microprocessor with 32-bit register, a 16-bit data bus, and a 24-bit address bus. It can operate in real, protected, and virtual real mode. This processor was designed as a low-cost version of the 80386.
ANSI	The American national Standards Institute. It has given its name to a file that gives standard sequences for controlling the display, among other aspects of a computer system. See ANSI.SYS.
ANSI.SYS	A file of standard settings that can be used in your CONFIG.SYS file, by adding the line: device = ANSI.SYS. Your computer can then use the standard ANSI

sequences for changing what each key stroke does, for example.

APPLICATION Now usually a computer program that applies your computer to a specific task, such as word processing.

ARCHITECTURE The way in which the computer has been put together at a conceptual level. For example, the PC was created so that extra items could be added to it, such as modems, hard disk and tape streams. See Open Architecture.

ASCII The American Standards for Character Information and Interchange. This is a standard list character codes which gives each character a set position in a table of characters, known as the ASCII Table. In the normal ASCII set, there are 128 characters, numbered from 0 to 127.. The PC, however, also supports an extended ASCII character set, numbered from 0 to 255, making 256 characters in all. The self give you accented letters and line drawing characters as well.

ATTRIBUTES Usually says what condition applies to elements like files and characters. For example, whether a file is read only.

AUTOEXEC.BAT A special batch file which DOS looks for when you boot the system. It can be used to set the system up automatically.

BATCH A special file which you can call by typing its name, without its extension which is always .bat. It can contain a number of commands in sequence.

BOOTING The term getting the machine working with MS-DOS or another operating

	system. (See, Cold and Boot and Warm Boot).
CLUSTER	A cluster is one or more disk sectors addressed by the Operating System as one unit when reading from or writing to the disk.
COLD BOOT	Booting the machine by turning it on and getting it working from scratch. (Booting and Warm Booting).
COMMAN	An instruction which is recognized by MS-DOS as a specific task to be undertaken, like copy. Alternatively, the common interpreter.
COMMAND LINE PROMPT	See Prompt.
CONFIG.SYS	A special file which sets MS-DOS upto individual requirements.
[Ctrl]-[Alt]-[Del]	Three keys which when pressed together will cause the system to reboot.
CURSOR	A symbol, sometimes flashing, which indicated the point on the screen at which output or input will be displayed.
CYLINDER	A pair of tracks on opposite sides of a disk.
DATABASE	Either a file which holds in a certain format, such as lists of customers and accounts, or the application program used to create such a file.
DEFAULT	The value that any of the variable settings under MS-DOS has when you boot the system.
DENSITY	Floppy disks can be single, double or quadruple density, depending on the

	number of tracks per inch that they can hold.
DEVICE	Software or hardware that can be used as part of the computer system, for example, a printer or the file ANSI.SYS.
DEVICE DRIVER	Software which handles the communication between the main computer board and Devices.
DIRECTORY	A list of files or a special file which holds the names of files on a disk.
ENVIRONMENT	This is the memory area that is allocated by MS-DOS for the user to define certain functions, such as the path MS-DOS will use.
EXTENSION	The last three letters of a file name following a full stop or period.
EXTERNAL COMMAND	A command that has to be loaded as a separate program when you want to use it.
FILE	Either a collection of data or a piece of hardware that is treated as a collection of data by MS-DOS, for example, a printer.
FILE NAME	The name given to a file.
HIDDEN FILES	Files held on a disk which do not appear in a directory when it is listed.
I/O	Input/Output. A circuit path allows independent communications between the processor and external devices.
IBMBIO.COM	One of the DOS system files required to boot the system. This is the first file loaded from disk during the boot, and it contains extension to the ROM BIOS.

IBMDOS.COM   One of the DOS system files to boot the machine. This file contains the primary DOS routines. Loaded by IBMBIO.COM. It in turn loads COMMAND.COM.

INTERNAL COMMAND   A command that is always available whenever you have the command line prompt. DIR and COPY are two examples of internal commands.

LAN   Local Area Network, A group of computers in fairly close proximity which are connected together to share common resource.

LOCAL RESOURCES   Resources which exist on the computer system itself.

LOGICAL   If something is logical to MS-DOS, it does not actually exist, but MS-DOS treats it as though it does, for example, a logical disk drive created by the command subset.

LOGICAL DRIVE   A drive as named by a DOS drive specifier, such as C: or D:. Under DOS 3.3 or later, a single physical drive may act as several logical drives, each with its own specifier.

LOW LEVEL FORMATTING   Formatting that divides tracks into sectors on the parallel surfaces. This type of format will place sector identifying information before and after each sector and fill each sector with null data (usually hex F6). In this format, the sector interleave is specified and defective tracks are marked. A defective track is marked when invalid checksum figures are placed in each sector on a defective track.

MEMORY   A service provided by a extremely fast

177

CACHING	memory chips that keeps copies of the most recent memory accessed. When the CPU marks a subsequent access, the value is supplied by the fast memory rather than from relatively slow system memory.
MEMORY RESIDENT	Programs which once loaded remain in memory at all times, even when other program are being run. Such programs can generally be called up directly by a combination of keys.
MOUSE	A device for pointing, held in the hand and rolled on a flat surface which in turn moves the cursor. It can have one, two or three buttons which act like certain keys such as (Return).
MULTITASKING	The act of running several programs simultaneously.
MULTI-USER SYSTEM	A system in which several computer terminals share the name CPU.
NETWORK	The way that two or more computers are linked together so that they can share common resources.
OPEN ARCHITECTURE	A machine is said to have open architecture if it has been designed to make it easy for extra facilities and function to be built in.
OPERATING SYSTEM	A program which controls the operation of the computer and handles the input and output routines.
PARTITION	A section of a hard disk devoted to a particular Operating System. Most hard disks have only one partition, devoted to DOS. A hard disk can have upto four partitions. Each occupied by a different

	Operating System. DOS 3.3 or higher can occupy two of these four partitions.
PATH NAME	The full name of a file including all directories and sub-directories that hold it, starting at the current directory or from the root directory.
PERIPHERAL	Any piece of equipment used in computer systems that is an attachment to the computer itself. Disk drives, terminals, and printers are all examples of peripherals.
PHYSICAL	Physical means that it is actually there, as opposed to either logical or virtual.
PHYSICAL DRIVE	A single disk drive. DOS defines logical drives, which are given a specifier. Such as C: or D:. A single physical drive may be divided multiple logical drives. Conversely, special software can span a single logical drive across two physical drives.
PRIMARY PARTITION	Starting with DOS 3.3, a hard disk may have two partitions that serve DOS- a primary partition, which is an ordinary, single-volume bootable partition, and an extended partition, which may contain any number of volumes upto 23 in total. Using both partitions, a single disk can be divided into 24 volumes.
PROMPT	A message or symbol indicating that the computer is ready to receive commands.
PROGRAM	A set of instructions which the computer will follow.
PROGRAM FILE	A file which contains instructions which from a program and which will be run upon loading into the computer.

RAM DISK	An area of memory which is treated by MS-DOS as a disk drive.
READ ONLY	An attribute that prevents a device being written to.
REMOTE RESOURCES	Resources which exist on a computer other than the one on which they are being invoked.
RESOURCES	Facilities made use of by the computer, which can be either internal, such as directories and drives, or external such as printers The term is mostly used in conjunction with networks.
ROOT	The first directory on a disk form which all references to sub-directories are made.
SECTOR	A division of a track on a disk.
SECTOR	A computer on a network which administers, controls and allocates resources.
SPREADSHEET	An application program which allows you to enter numbers and values and relate them to each other visually.
SUB-DIRECTORY	A directory which belongs to and is held within another directory.
SWITCH	A single letter following a slash, which alters the way a command works, for example's following format.
SYSTEM	Everything that forms part of the computer, including printers if they are attached, for example.
SYSTEM FILE	A file containing either data or code used by the Operating System as part of its normal operation.

TPI	Tracks Per Inch. Used as a measurement of magnetic track density. Standard 5 1/4-inch 360 K floppy disks have a 48 TPI density, and the 1.2M disks have a 96 TPI density. All 3 1/2 inch disks have a 135 TPI density, and hard disks can have densities greater than 1,000 TPI.
TRACK	One of the many concentric circles that hold data on a disk surface. A track consists of a single line of magnetic flux changes. A number of tracks are on a disk, and information is written onto the tracks. Each track is divided into some number of sectors, each of which is 512 bytes long.
UTILITY PROGRAM	Application programs which provide resources for handling the system but do not form part of MS-DOS.
VIRTUAL	Something that is not actually physically present, but which is almost identical in operation to what is describing, like a window of the screen which is referred to as a virtual screen.
VIRTUAL DISK	A "phantom disk drive" by which a section of system memory (usually RAM) is set aside to hold data, just as if it were a number of disk sectors. To DOS a virtual disk looks like and functions like any other "real" drive Synonymous with RAM disk.
WARM BOOT	This generally means rebooting the machine without losing, say, the position you are in a program. Under MS-DOS this is not possible, and term is used to describe rebooting using a software

	routing, by for example, pressing [Ctrl+1] - [Alt] - [Del].
WORD PROCESSOR	An application program which provides facilities for the input, processing, storage and output of text-based documents.
WORKSTATION	A computer on a network which can be used to access the network resources, without necessarily having any independent resources of its own.

APPENDIX F
ADVANCE DOS TOPICS

ANTI-VIRUS DETECTION AND CLEANING

More than 1,000 computer virus exist that can damage both data files and computer programs. MS-DOS 6.00 includes anti-virus utilities that scan your drives for virus-infected files. A virus signature file is supplied which identifies common viruses.

WHICH ANTI-VIRUS PROGRAM DO I HAVE ?

One anti-virus program is designed to run directly from the MS-DOS prompt. Another runs from Windows. s There is also a memory-resident program, called VSAFE, that can be loaded for monitoring incoming files for virus infection. VSAFE can be loaded directly from the DOS prompt. To use it with Windows, a VSafe manager named MWAVTSR.EXE is loaded. When you installed DOS 6 using SETUP, you were given the opportunity to load either or both versions of the anti-virus utility. This section describes the use of both.

To determine which anti-virus software you have availableon your hard disk, checkyour C:\DOS directory for one of the following files :

MWAV.EXE   Microsoft Windows anti-virus program

MSAV.EXE   MS-DOS anti-virus program

VSAFE.EXE   A memory-resident virus protection program that scans files before they are copied to your drive.

MWAVTSR.EXE   A VSafe Manager used by Windows. This file is called either from the Windows initialization file, WIN.INI, by adding the filename to the load = line. If you use

444

Windows 3.1, the MWAVTSR.EXE file is added to the Windows Startup group.

You'll also notice a number of companion files that begin with either MWAV or MSAW. These are used by the executable files listed above. The MWAVTSR.EXE program file is the memory-resident utility mentioned above.

THE MS-DOS ANTI-VIRUS PROGRAM

An Anti-Virus screen is displayed when you type MSAV and press Enter. The menu selections are picked using the Arrow keys. Once highlighted, press Enter to activate. A prompt line at the bottom of the screen accesses selections plus help using function keys F1 through F9. Each selection is briefly described in the text box at the right side of the screen. The selections are summarized below.

Detect

Scan the current drive for virus detection. Upon virus detection, you can clean the file, continue without cleaning, or exit the detection process. F4 also starts the Detect Selection.

Detect and Clean

Scan the current drive for virus detection. Upon virus detection, the file is automatically cleaned. Scanning resumes automatically. F5 also starts the Detect and Clean selection.

Select new drive

Provides the ability to scan other drives by displaying a drive selection line. Type the drive designator, such as A or C, and press Enter. F2 also starts the Select new drive selection.

Options

Displays an Options dialog box which is used to configure the way the program works. F8 also displays the Options dialog box. Options include :

Verify integrity Alerts you for changes in executable files based on information contained in the CHKLIST.MS file, which was created during a prior scan when Create New Checksums was active. This is a defense against possible new, unknown viruses.

Create New Checksums

When active, this option creates a checklist file, named CHKLIST.MS, which retains checksum information about each executable file that is scanned. Checksum information includes file attributes, size, date and time.

Create Checksums on Floppy

When this option and the Create New Checksums option are both active, the CHKLIST.MS file is created for a scanned floppy diskette.

Disable Alarm Sound

This option turns off the "beep" when a warning message is displayed.

Create Backup This option creates a backup file of the infected file before it is cleaned. The backup file assumes the extension VIR. This is a risky option, as the virus remains on your disk as long as the infected file exists.

Create Report Creates an ASCII text report file named MSAV.RPT. The report summarizes the number of boot sector and file viruses found and removed.

Prompt while Detect

Displays a dialog box each time aninfected file is detected.

Anti-Stealth   A stealth virus changes an executable file internally without affecting its external appearance. The Anti-Stealth option, working in conjunction with Verify Integrity, is used to detect stealth viruses.

Check All Files   Normally, just executable files are checked. This option checks all file types for infection.

Exit   Used to exit the program. Pressing F3 is also used to exit.

Other Function Keys :

F1   Press F1 to display help information about each of the dialog box selections.

F7   Press F7 to delete any checklist files that were previously created during scan.

F9   Press F9 to display a list of virus names recognized by the anti-virus program.

WHEN A VIRUS IS DETECTED

When a virus is detected, a "Virus Found" message is displayed. If the virus signature matches one supplied, the virus name is displayed. If the file is destroyed by the virus, the system tells you that the file is not recoverable. At this point you should delete the infected file by choosing the Delete button. There are times when a file is cleaned but does not operate following the clean operation. When this occurs, delete the suspect file and replace it with the equivalent file on your original program source diskette. This may require that you reinstall the entire program.

However, finding and eliminating the virus will prevent it from infecting other software.

VIRUS SAFE (VSAFE)

The VSAFE command was introduced with the releaseof MS-DOS 6.00. VSAFE is a memory-resident anti-virus utility that monitors files for possible virusinfection. When loaded into memory, VSAFE consukes about 44 K of total memory. Generally, it uses about 23K of conventional memory and 23K of upper memory.

If an unusual condition is detected, VSAFE alerts you to the condition.   VSAFE is used with either DOS or Windows operation.   The technique for loading VSAFE varies with DOS and Windows.

USING VSAFE WITH DOS

To run the VSAFE program with dOS, type VSAFE andpress Enter at the DOS prompt. VSAFE loads into your computer's memory. If you want to load it each time you turn on your computer, add the command VSAFE to your AUTOEXEC.BAT file. You may wish to use one of the switches /NE, /NX, /Cx, etc. described by the DOS help system. Simply type HELP VSAFE and press Enter to see a description of each switch. Note that /Cx and /Ax change the hotkeys, which is the key sequence used to display the dialog box. Alt-V is the default. You may wish tochange the hot key if it conflicts with a key sequence used by one of your application programs.

Warning Types

1. HD Low Level Format   Alerts you when a pending formatting operation could erase all data on the designated disk.

2. Resident   Alerts you when a program attempts to stay resident in memory. This does not necessarily indicate the presence of a virus.

3. General Write Protect   Prevents a program from writing to disk, which prevents a virus from infecting the active disk.

4. Check executable files   Checks programs that are opened by MS-DOS.

5. Boot sector viruses   Checks your disks for possible boot sector viruses.

6. Protect HD boot sector   Alerts you of any attempts to write to the hard disk boot sector and partition table.

7. Protect FD boot sector   Alerts you of any attempts to write to a floppy disk boot sector.

8. Protect executable files   Alerts you of attempts to modify executable files.

Changing Settings

To change the ON/OFF setting of any of the eight checks, press Alt-V to display the dialog box. Then type the indicated number 1 through 8. Type the number again to toggle it back to the original setting.

Exiting the Dialog Box

To hide the dialog box, press Esc. VSAFE continues operation using the settings established upon exit.

Unloading VSAFE From Memory

To unload VSAFE from memory, display the dialog box with Alt-V. Once displayed, press Alt-U to unload VSAFE. Once unloaded, the memory used is returned for use.

APPENDIX G
What's New in MS-DOS 6.22?

ENHANCEMENTS TO DISK COMPRESSION

➜ MS-DOS 6.0 and 6.2 included DoubleSpace disk compression. MS-DOS 6.22 includes DriveSpace compression instead of DoubleSpace. DriveSpace appears similar to DoubleSpace, but stores compressed information in a different format. (If you are currently using DoubleSpace, you can continue to use it with MS-DOS 6.22. For more information, see <DBLSPACE>).

➜ DriveSpace includes several new safety and convenience features that were not in MS-DOS 6 DoubleSpace (if you are still using DoubleSpace with MS-DOS 6.22, Setup has also made these enhancements to DoubleSpace):

➜ DoubleGuard safety checking, which protects against data corruption by verifying data integrity before writing data to your disk. If DoubleGuard detects that the memory DriveSpace is using has been corrupted by another program, it shuts down your computer immediately to minimize damage to your data.

OTHER ENHANCEMENTS

➜ MS-DOS 6.22 includes ScanDisk, a utility that detects, diagnoses, and repairs disk errors on both uncompressed and compressed drives. ScanDisk can repair file system errors (such as crosslinks and lost clusters) and physical disk errors. ScanDisk keeps a log of its repairs and enables you to undo any of the changes it made. DriveSpace runs ScanDisk to check the reliability of your disk before it begins compression. You can also run ScanDisk yourself by

→ typing SCANDISK at the command prompt. For more information, see <An Introduction to ScanDisk>.

→ The MS-DOS extended-memory manager, HIMEM, automatically tests your system's memory when you start your computer. This test can identify memory chips that are no longer reliable. (Unreliable memory can result in system instability or loss of data.) To turn off the memory test, add the / TESTMEM:OFF switch to the command that starts HIMEM. For more information, see <HIMEM.SYS>.

→ Setup now configures SMARTDrive as a read-only cache by default. Even if write-caching is enabled, MS-DOS does not display the command prompt until SMARTDrive has written its cache to your disk. This prevents you from turning off your computer before the data in memory is saved.

→ The <MOVE>, <COPY>, and <XCOPY> commands now ask you for confirmation before copying a file over another file that has the same name. (However, when issued from a batch file, these commands do not prompt for confirmation before overwriting a file.)

EASE-OF-USE FEATURES

→ You can now bypass or carry out individual commands in your AUTOEXEC.BAT and other batch programs. (In MS-DOS 6, this capability was limited to your CONFIG.SYS file.) This feature makes it easier to isolate problems when you are troubleshooting problems in your system configuration or in batch programs.

→ To step through the commands in your AUTOEXEC.BAT file, press F8 when your computer starts. For more information, see "Bypassing CONFIG.SYS and AUTOEXEC.BAT Commands" in the <CONFIG.SYS Commands> topic. To step through other batch files, use the <COMMAND /Y> command.

➔ The <DISKCOPY> command now uses your hard disk as an interim storage area, which makes copying from one floppy disk to another faster and easier.

➔ Microsoft Defragmenter makes better use of your computer's extended memory, so it can now defragment much larger disks and disks containing many more files and directories. For more information on running Defragmenter, see the <DEFRAG> command.

➔ The output of the DIR, MEM, CHKDSK, and FORMAT commands is much easier to read, since it now includes thousands separators when displaying numbers greater than 999. For example, "1000000 bytes free" now reads "1,000,000 bytes free."

DBLSPACE

Manages compressed data disks.

Syntax

DBLSPACE / switches drive:

The first time you invoke DBLSPACE, it runs through an automatic self-configuration routine. it compresses the data on a drive that you select, usually drive c . The process takes a significant amount of time. During the process, DBLSPACE re-starts your computer twice.

Compressed data drives appear to function just like uncompressed drives; the process of handeling compressed dat is completely transparent to the user.

After DBLSPACE has configured itself, you can invoke the DBLSPACE command to manage certain functions of your compressed drive.

Switches

drive: Displays information about a drive.

/AUTOMOUNT = 0	Disables automatic mounting of compressed floppy drives. Because this switch modifies the DBLSPACE initialization file, you must reboot the computer for this feature to take effect.
/AUTOMOUNT = 1	Enables automounting of all compressed floppy drives.
/AUTOMOUNT = drives	
	Enables automatic mounting of specific compressed floppy drives, where drives are the letters of the drives to be mounted.
/CHKDSK drive:	Checks the compressed disk for errors on drive. If no error is found, no message is displayed.
/COMPRESS drive:	Compress an existing drive.
/DEFRAGMENT drive:	Rewrite files on the compressed drive in contiguous sectors.
/DELETE drive:	Delete compressed drive. All files are lost.
/FORMAT drive:	Reformat compressed drive. All files are lost.
/MOUNT=nnn drive:	Connects a compressed volume to drive letter drive, where nnn is the number of the compressed volume file.
/MOUNT = nnn/NEW- DRIVE = new: drive:	Connects a compressed volume to drive letter drive, and assigns new drive letter new.nnn is the number of the compressed volume file.
/RATIO = n.nn drive:	Assigns a new compression ratio to compressed drive.

| /SIZE = n.nn drive: | Changes the size of drive, where n.nn is the new drive size. |
| /UMOUNT drive: | Disconnects drive from its compressed volume file. |

E.g.　　DBLSPACE /COMPRESS D:

Changes existing disk D: to a compressed drive, using default size and compression ratio.

DBLSPACE /MOUNT=001 /A:

Connects the compressed floppy drive in A: to compressed volume 001.

DBLSPACE /UMOUNT A:

Disconnects the compressed floppy drive in A:

DEFRAG

Syntax

DEFRAG drive: /switches

As the hard disk is used the files becomes fragmented. this means that they are broken into sections and scattered in disparate areas of the disk. DEFRAG optimizes diek performance by arranging these fragmented files in contiguous sectors. This makes file reading faster and saves wear & tear on a disk's moving parts.

If the DEFRAG command is invoked without the drive: parameter, you are presented with a full screen, menu-driven system. The drives to be optimized can be selected from the options available.

DEFRAG includes an extensive online help system. to access on-line help, press F1.

| /F | Arranges defragmented files. |
| /U | Does not reallocate defragmented files. |

/S:order	Sorts the files in their directories, according to the value of order, which can be one or more of the following characters.

        N = Alphabetically by name

        N- = Reverse-Alphabetically by name.

        E = Alphabetically by extension.

        E- = Reverse-alphabetically by extension

        D = Date/Time, ascending

        D- = Date/time, descending

        S = Size, smallest to largest

        S- = Size, largest to smallest.

/B	Restart the computer after defragmentation.
/V	Verifies the defragmented files match the original file image in memory.
/SKIPHIGH	Forces DEFRAG to run from conventional memory.

E.g.   **DEFRAG c: /F /S:SDS**

defragmented files and sorts them on disk so that no empty spaces fall between them, and arranges them in directories by extension.

SCANDISK

Analyzes and repairs logical and physical disk errors. This command is available in Ver 6.2 & later.

Syntax

SCANDISK drive: /switches

SCANDISK can fix errors on commnly used data storage devices such as hard-disk and floppy disks, RAM drives, and DBLSPACE compressed drives.

SCANDISK analyzes and repairs damage to the following:

* Physical cluster
* File Allocation Table (FAT)
* Lost cluster
* Croee-linked files
* Directory tree
* MS-DOS boot sector

The drive parameter indicates the drive to be scanned, where drive is the letter of the disk drive.

Switches

/ALL	Checks and repairs all non network drives
/AUTOFIX	Supresses prompts to fix errors.
/CHECKONLY	Scans but not fix errors.
/CUSTOM	Process using special configuration instructions found in SCANDISK.INI.
/NOSAVE	Forces deletion of lost clusters. The default setting saves lost cluster in files on the root directory.
/NOSUMMARY	Supresses display of statistical summary at the conclusion of scan and repair.
/SURFACE	Performs a surface scan, seeking bad cluster on physical surface of the disk.
/UNDO drive:	Restores a disk to its previous state, using the special "UNDO disk" that you were prompted to create during the repair process.

E.g.   **SCANDISK C: /NOSAVE /SURFACE**

scans and repairs errors on drive C, automatically deletes any lost clusters, and automatically begains a surface scan after scanning for logical errors.

MEMMAKER

Automatically configures your system's device drivers to optimize random-access memory(RAM).

Syntax

MEMMAKER /switches

MEMMAKER analyzes your current system configuration and rewrite CONFIG.SYS and AUTOEXEC.BAT to make optimal use of your system's random-access memory(RAM).

MEMMAKER will restart your computer twice during processing.

Switches

/BATCH	Runs unattended (batch mode). MemMaker assumes default response for all prompts.
/UNDO	Undo the most recent changes made by MEMMAKER. Restart MEMMAKER using this switch if your system doesn't work properly after MEMMAKER completes.
/W: size1, size2	Specifies the amount of upper-memory space for Windows translation buffers. Windows requires two regions in upper memory for these buffers. while size1 is the first region, size2 is the second, in kilobytes.

E.g. MEMMAKER /BATCH

starts MEMMAKER in batch mode, and automatically rewrites system configuration files using all default responses for your system.

EXERCISE

1. The "DIR" command displays
    a) Filename,Extension,Size,Date,Time.
    b) Filename,Extension,Date,Size,Time.
    c) Filename,Extension,Date,Time,Size.
    d) Filename,Extension,Time,Date,Size.

2. The last line of "DIR" command displays
    a) Size of files in Bytes of "directory"
    b) Size of files in KiloBytes of"directory"
    c) Total amount of disk space used in Bytes.
    d) None of the above.

3. One Mb is
    a) 1048576 bytes.   b) 1048000 bytes.
    c) 1024000 bytes.   d) 1024576 bytes.

4. The "DIR" command display files sorted on
    a) Name.   b) Extension.
    c) Size.   d) Date/Time.
    e) None of the above.

5. The "?" in DOS" means
    a) One and only One character.
    b) One character.
    c) Zero or One character.
    d) Less than One.

6. "*"in DOS means:
    a) Zero or more characters
    b) Atleast two characters.
    c) Any one characters.
    d) One and more characters.

7. A files in DOS has the following properties
    a) Filename Seven characters and Extension Four.
    b) Filename Eight characters and Extension Three.

c) Filename Seven characters and Extension Five.

d) Filename Eleven characters and Extension Zero.

e) None of the above.

8. If you use the following command to create a file with an extension of 4 characters what will be the resultant extension?

   C:\> COPY CON ABC.ATXT

   a) File creation error.

   b) Extension is truncated to Three

   c) Extension is left as Four characters.

   d) None of the above.

9. If you have 512 files in the root directory and you try to copy a 513th files what will be the error message display?

   a) No error message.

   b) File creation error.

   c) File cannot be copied on to itself.

   d) None of the above.

10. The maxinum number of files in a sub-directory can be:

   a) As many as you like.

   b) 512 Files.

   c) Depending on the free space available on the hard disk.

   d) None of the above.

11. Which of the following files are a must for the booting process to complete?

   a) CONFIG.SYS. & IO.SYS.

   b) AUTOEXEC.BAT,CONFIG.SYS & MSDOS.SYS.

   c) COMMAND.COM. & MSDOS.SYS.

   d) MSDOS.SYS. & IO.SYS.

   e) MSDOS.SYS.IO.SYS. & ANY DOS SHELL.

12. After the command " DEL*.* " is given,the following message is displayed:

Are you sure (Y/N)?

What happens if the answer you key in is "Q"?

a) Quits & returns to DOS prompt.

b) Quits out of sub-directory.

c) Deletes all the files.

d) Message appears again.

e) None of the above.

13. If your system has only one floppy disk drive, what will the following command display?

C:\>DIR B:

a) Drive B: not found.

b) Not ready error reading Drive B:

c) Insert diskette in drive B: and strike any key when ready.

d) Gives you all the files in drive B:

e) None of the above.

14. What will the following command do?

C:\WS>COPY.*TXT D:

a) Copy all files with extension "TXT" from D:to C:

b) Copy all files from D: root directory,to C:

c) Returns an error message.

d) Copy all files with the extension "TXT" from current directory of C: to D: root directory.

e) None of the above.

15. To display the contents of the root directory of drive C from A drive would say:

a) DIR C: b) DIR

c) DIR C:\   d) DIR *.*

e) None of the above.

16. If with the "CD" command you get an error, where do you go?

a) Parent directory.

b) Root directory.

c) You remain where you were.

d) None of the above.

17. What is the error message displayed if you try create a directory using already existing directory name?

a) Directory already exists.

b) Bad command or file file name.

c) No error message is displayed.

d) Unable to create directory.

e) None of the above.

18. What is the effect of using the following command?

C:\MD WS

a) Directory already exists.

b) Bad command or file name.

c) A new sub-directory with the name WS is created.

d) Unable to create directory.

e) None of the above.

19. What happens if you try to remove (delete)a sub-directory which is not empty?

a) Error message "Bad command of file name".

b) The files as well as the sub-directory name are removed.

c) Error message"Invalid path, not directory, or directory not empty."

d) No error message and returns to DOS prompt.

e) None of the above.

20. What happens if you try to remove (delete) a sub-directory which is empty?

a) Error message"Bad command or file name".

b) The files as well as the sub-directroy name are removed.

c) Error message"Invalid path,not directory, ordirectory not empty."

d) No error message and returns to DOS prompt.

e) None of the above.

21. What is the effect of giving the following command?

    C\DBASE>RD DBASE

    a) The sub-directory"DBASE" is removed and you come to the root directory.

    b) The sub-directory "DBASE" is removed and the System hangs.

    c) The System hangs.

    d) "Invalid path,not directory, or directory not empty

    e) None of the above.

22. What does the command do?

    PROMPTPG

    a) The prompt changes to$P$G.

    b) Error Message"Bad command or file name".

    c) Error prompt shows you the current drive,a"\" and a">".eg:C:\>

    d) The prompt shows you date and time.

    e) None of the above.

23. What does the command do?

    C:\PROMPT$D$T

    a) The prompt changes to DT.

    b) Error message"Bad command of file name".

    c) Error message"Invalid number of parameters".

    d) The prompt shows you the current drive a"\" and a">"e.g. C:\>

    e) The prompt shows you date and time.

    f) None of the above.

24. What happens if you enter the wrong time format while using the "TIME" command?

a) The System retains the old date and retains to the DOS prompt.

b) The system reboots.

c) You are prompted to re-enter a valid time.

d) None of the above.

25. What is the effect of the following command?

   A:\>FORMAT

a) Formats A drive.

b) Formats C drive.

c) Returns back to DOS prompt.

d) "Drive letter must be spacified".

e) None of the above.

26. What will happen if the following lines are there in "CONFIG.SYS"?

   Line1   DEVICE = C:\ANSI.SYS

   Line 2 DEVICE = C:\ANSI.SYS

a) The device driver "ANSI.SYS" is loaded twice

b) Displays "Unrecognized command in CONFIG.SYS"

c) The system hangs

d) It displays an error message and reboots the System

e) None of the above.

27. In DOS what does "FAT" stands for?

a) FILE ATTRIBUTE TABLE

b) FILE ALLOCATED TABLE

c) FILE ALLOCATION TABLE

d) FILE ALLOCATION TABLE

e) FILE ASSIGNMENT TABLE

28. When you copy one file to another, what date & time will the new file will have?

a) Current date & time is copied to both file

b) Current date time is copied to destination file

c) Current date & time is copied to the source file

202

    d) Date & time of source file is copied to destination file.

29. To display the contents of the root directory from within a sub-directory, you would say

    a) DIR C: b) DIR

    c) DIR C:\   d) DIR *.*

30. What do the first two enteries "." (single dot) & ".." (double dot) in a directory listing signify in a sub-directory?

    a) Special files   b) Directories

    c) Hidden files   d) None of the above.

31. What is the meaning of "/t:yy" in the "FORMAT" utility?

    a) Formats the diskette with "yy" sectors per track

    b) Formats the diskette with "yy" tracks

    c) Format takes the value of "yy" to be size of the floppy diskette to be formatted

    d) Formats the disk taking the value of "yy" and the capacity of the floppy

32. Which of the following seperators can be used in the "PATH" variable?

    a) ":"   b) ","

    c) ";"   d) "/"

33. What does CHKDSK utility of DOS do?

    a) Checks the volume label of the disk

    b) Checks if the disk is bootable

    c) Checks if the disk has a partition table

    d) Gives you a whole lot of details of your disk like size, number of lost chains or clusters, total disk space free, number of directories present

    e) Checks if a hard disk is present in your system

34. What will the following batch command do?

    FOR %1 IN (*.TXT) DO TYPE %1

    a) It displays all the files with .TXT extension

b) It will type out all the files in that sub-directory or root

c) It will type out all the files with .TXT extension present in that particular sub-directory or root directory.

d) None of the above

35. What will the following command result in?

C:\> COPY FILE1 +FILE2

a) Overwrite contents of FILE1 with contents of FILE2

b) Overwrite contents of FILE2 with content of FILE1.

c) Append contents of FILE1 to the contents of FILE2

d) Append contents of FILE2 to the contents of FILE1

e) None of the above

36. What does the following command result in?

(Assuming that there is a file called "DOSTEXT.TXT" in your current directory or drive)

C:\> Type DOSTEST.TXT | MORE

a) Returns an error message

b) Returns an error message saying "Unknown symbol | in command"

c) Displays 23 lines of file and says -MORE- till end of file is displayed

d) Displays 24 lines of file and says -MORE- till end of file is displayed

e) None of the above

37. The /+n switch of the SORT command

a) Sorts only those lines specified by numer n

b) Sorts lines starting with the contents specified in column n

c) Sorts in numerical order

d) Sort does not recognize this switch

38. What is the best way to echo a blank line on the screen?

a) ECHO followed by 80 spaces

b) Just ECHO

c) ECHO, one space and then the ASCII character value for 255

d) ECHO followed by two spaces

39. What value does parameter %0 take in a batch file?

a) The first parameter that you have typed

b) The last parameter that you have typed

c) There is no parameter like %0

d) The name of the batch file

40. What happens when you give the following lines in CONFIG.SYS (Assuming that you have only 1 MB of RAM)

Line1   DEVICE = C:\DOS\HIMEM.SYS

Line 2 DOS = HIGH

a) DOS is loaded as high memory driver

b) Higher portion of DOS is loaded in memory

c) DOS is loaded in HIGH MEMORY AREA

d) Error message "HMA not available; loading DOS low"

e) Extended Memory is made available and then some part within 1Mb is made as High Memory Area and then DOS is loaded there.

41. What happens when you give the foloowing lines in CONFIG.SYS?

(Assuming that yoou have 4Mb of RAM)

Line 1   DEVICE = C:\DOS\HIMEM.SYS

Line 2 DOS = HIGH

a) DOS is loaded as high memory driver

b) Higher portion of DOS is loaded in the memory

c) DOS is loaded in HIGH MEMORY AREA

d) Error Message "HMA Not available: Loading DOS low"

e) Error Message "EMM386 not installed - XMS manager not present" HMA not available : Loading DOS low"

42. The /E switch of COMMAND.COM is used for

   a) Run the Command interpreter in the extended memory

   b) Set the initial environment size to specified number of bytes

   c) Command interpreter should use expanded memory

   d) None of the above

43. What does UNDELETE/DT do?

   a) Shows all files available for undeletion with deletion-tracking

   b) Uses only deletion tracking files

   c) Invalid switch

   d) None of the above

44. What does the VER command do?

   a) It is the abbriviated form of VERIFY command

   b) Gives an error message

   c) Displays the version number of DOS which you are using

   d) None of the above

45. What facilities are provided if you include the following line in our CONFIG.SYS?

   Line 1 DEVICE = HIMEM.SYS

   a) It helps you to use expanded memory

   b) It helps you to use Extended memory

   c) It helps you to use Upper memory block

   d) It helps you to use High Memory Area

   e) It provides you an extra drive on your system in High Memory Area

46. What happens when you add the following line in your CONFIG.SYS?

    Line 1DEVICE = EMM386.SYS

    a) It helps you to use Expanded Memory

    b) It helps you to use Extended Memory

    c) It helps you to use High Memory Area

    d) It helps you to use Upper Memory Block

    e) It gives you an extra drive on your system

47. What happens if you include the following in your CONFIG.SYS

    DEVICE = RAMDRIVE.SYS 1024/E

    a) It helps you to use Hard disk as RAM

    b) It helps you to use floppy disk as RAM

    c) It converts ROM into RAM

    d) It is a driver to use blocks of 1024 bytes as Expanded RAM

    e) It gives you an extra drive on your system

48. Can you set PATH variable in CONFIG.SYS

    a) Yes   b) No

49. Is the following command valid, if drives A and B contain 360kB diskettes?

    C:\DOS> DISKCOPY A: B:

    a) Yes   b) No

50. Whenever you format a previously formatted floppy, Are you prompted for confirmation?

    a) Yes   b) No

51. Can you have a DOS System without a physical floppy drive connected but which has an hard disk?

    a) Yes   b) No

52. What is the effect of the following command?

    C:\WS>DEL A.TXT; B:TXT

    a) Only file A.TXT is deleted

b) Only file B.TXT is deleted

c) Both files are deleted

d) Message " Invalid number of parameters"

e) Message "File not found"

53. What happens when you type B: and press Enter, and there is no physical Drive B: on your system, and the PROMPT is set to pg?

    C:\DOS>B:

a) Takes you to Drive B: and displays B:\>

b) Displays Error message" No Drive found"

c) Insert diskette in drive B: and strike any key when ready

d) Remains in the drive you are in.

e) None of the above

54. What is the effect of giving the following command

    C:\DBASE>RD\DBASE

a) The directory is removed and you come to the root directory

b) The directory is removed and the system hangs

c) The system hangs

d) Error message "Invalid path, not directory, or directory not empty"

e) Error message "Invalid number of parameters"

55. Can you unhide IO.SYS and MSDOS.SYS files just by removing the HIDDEN attribute of those files?

a) YES   b) NO

56. What error message do you get if you have a blank file named "AUTOEXEC.BAT" in the root directory?

a) System will hang

b) Bad or missing AUTOEXEC.BAT

c) No error message

d) None of the above